OUT OF THE SHELL

OUT OF THE
SHELL

First published in 2012 by
New Holland Publishers
London • Sydney • Cape Town • Auckland
www.newhollandpublishers.com

Garfield House 86–88 Edgware Road London W2 2EA United Kingdom
1/66 Gibbes Street Chatswood NSW 2067 Australia
Wembley Square First Floor Solan Road Gardens Cape Town 8001 South Africa
218 Lake Road Northcote Auckland New Zealand

A catalogue record of this book is available at the British Library and the National Library of Australia.

ISBN: 9781742573595

Managing Director: Fiona Schultz
Designer: Stephanie Foti
Production Director: Olga Dementiev
Printer: Toppan Leefung Printing Limited

10 9 8 7 6 5 4 3 2 1

Follow New Holland Publishers on
Facebook: www.facebook.com/NewHollandPublishers

Contents

Introduction

Sensational shellfish

Ever taken a trip to the fish markets and been amazed by the range and variety of produce available? If you have always wanted to broaden your seafood cooking skills beyond fish and chips, then *Out of The Shell* is the cookbook you have been waiting for.

Shellfish and crustaceans, such as mussels, oysters, clams, prawns, scampi, lobsters and crabs, are nutritious, delicious, virtually fat free and relatively inexpensive. Although some varieties, such as crabs and lobster, require a little skill in preparation, it's not difficult to cook seafood. From a simple, traditional fisherman's chowder to a stunning lobster mornay, when it comes to seafood, the world really is your oyster.

From the novice cook to the pro, the recipes in *Out of The Shell* are simple to follow, and each section contains detailed information on how to buy, prepare and store your selected seafood. When it comes to seafood, the fresher the catch, the better the cooked result, although many frozen products offer great value and convenience. If you can, shop at fish markets where you can guarantee the freshness of the seafood on offer, and large supermarkets where the turn over is high. For the busy cook short of time but not prepared to compromise on quality, there are now a range of great convenience products, including already shelled prawns and cleaned mussels, ready to go straight into the pan.

Wherever possible, and to insure the freshest quality of your seafood, buy local products that are in-season and sustainably harvested. Shop around for the best produce and ask your fishmonger - they are more than happy to answer questions, give tips and even do some preparation for you. Most importantly, get together with family and friends, create a seafood feast and enjoy this wonderful harvest from the sea.

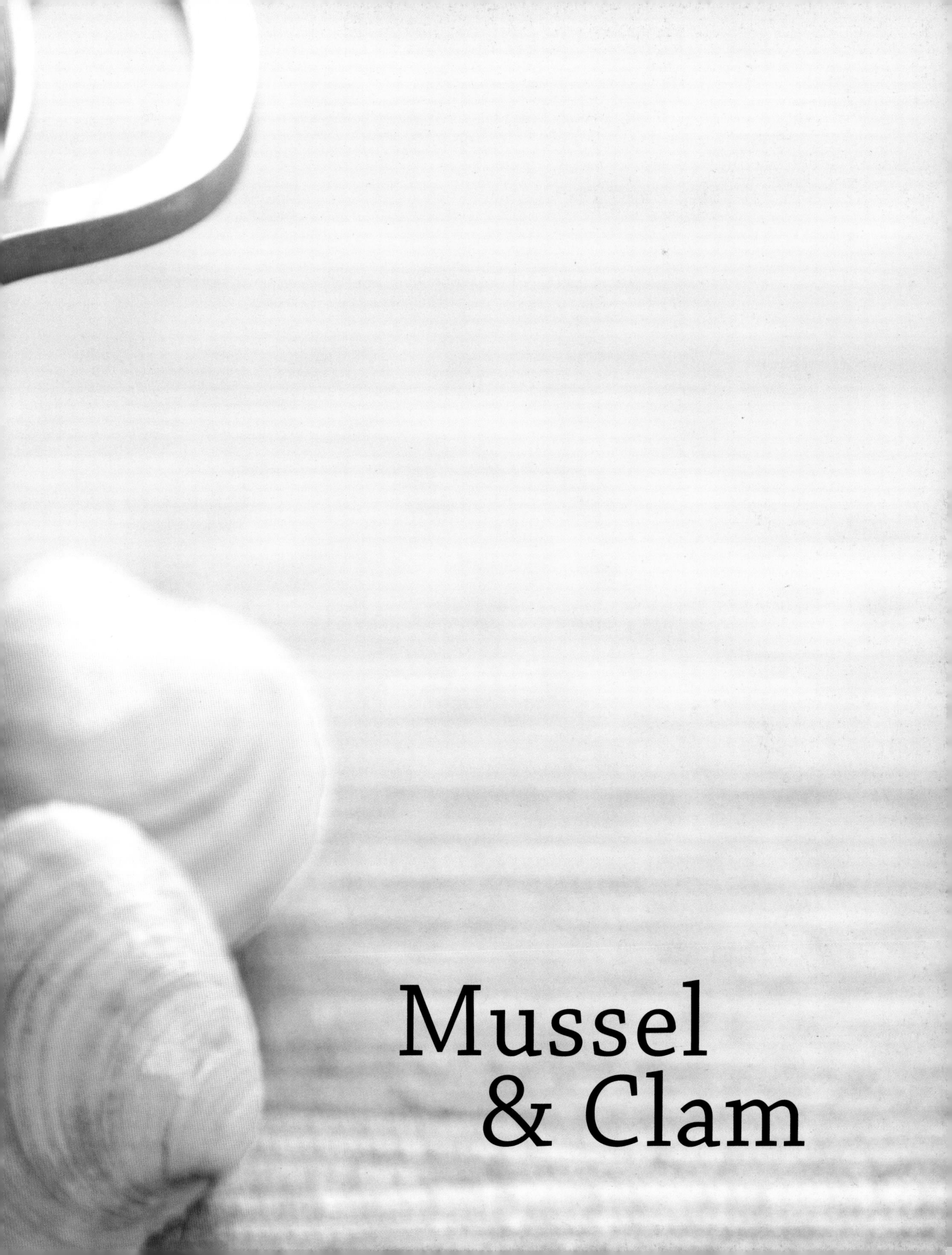

Mussel & Clam

Introduction

Mussels are part of a diverse group of molluscs which share the anatomical feature of a shell. While sometimes discarded in the creation of chowders, the shells of mussels have become an essential element in other recipes. They sustain the appearance of bite-size morsels. To many chefs, the shell is just as important as the flesh in the presentation of a unique culinary experience.

In their natural state, the shell of the mussel is sealed tight to guard against predators as well as the drying air during low tide. While the shells are commonly used in button making and the secreted pearls (usually of poorer quality than oysters) are found in inexpensive jewellery, it is the delicious visceral mass of the mussel that has intrigued seafood lovers worldwide.

Blended with exotic flavours, this magnificent mollusc can form the base of soups, salads, entrees or mains. A quick browse through this book will convince you of their versatility. Seasoned with the right combination of spices, the mussel can take on a brand new hue as well as an appetising new taste. The existence of mussels is common, but their application is broad.

This carefully selected collection of recipes is sure to cultivate a new appreciation for the mussel in even the most rigid diner. We have provided step-by-step instructions and beautiful illustrations to show you how easy it can be to impress your guests the next time you entertain. Remember that the presence of seafood on any table instantly lifts the standard of your meal. In particular, the mussel's neat, symmetrical shell and delectable taste embellish a dinner party with an upmarket ambience. Mussels simply look good and taste great. They are an easy choice and a guaranteed winner.

If this pleasure to the palate isn't enough to convince the uncertain, then the fact that the mussel has less fat that the average T-bone steak but is still full of nutrients will entice them. With so many reasons to make the mussel an addition to your list of food favourites, come out of your shell and discover a delectable delight from the deep blue.

San Franciscan Seafood Chowder

Serves 8

8 smallish round loaves of bread
55g/2oz butter
2 leeks, rinsed and finely sliced
2 onions, finely chopped
4 cloves garlic, minced
2 carrots, peeled and chopped
1 parsnip, peeled and chopped
2 stalks celery, finely sliced
1 tablespoon fresh thyme leaves
½ cup plain flour
8 cups fish stock
1kg/2lbs mixed seafood (including prawns/shrimp, mussels, clams, calamari/squid, white fish
200mL/7fl oz thickened cream
1 cup fresh parsley, chopped
salt and pepper, to taste
juice of 1 large lemon
½ bunch chives, chopped, for garnish

Preheat the oven to 200°C/400°F. First, prepare bread for bowls. Using a sharp knife, cut a large hole in the top of the bread loaf, then remove this crusty top and set aside. Carefully remove all the soft bread from the inside of the loaf (leaving the surrounding crust intact).

Place the loaves in the preheated oven and bake for 15 minutes (until the loaves are crisp and dry). Set aside.

Melt the butter in a large saucepan and add the leeks, onions, garlic, carrots, parsnip, celery and thyme leaves. Sauté for 10 minutes until the vegetables are soft and golden. Remove the pan from the heat and sprinkle flour over the vegetables, stirring constantly to mix flour with the butter. Return the pan to the heat and continue stirring until the mixture begins to turn golden (about 2 minutes). This gives the flour a 'cooked' flavour.

Add the fish stock stirring constantly to dissolve the roux mixture into the liquid, then simmer the soup for 20 minutes. Meanwhile, prepare the seafood by cutting the fish and shellfish into bite-sized pieces.

Add all the seafood, cream, parsley and salt and pepper, and cook for a further 5 minutes. (Do not allow the soup to boil rapidly because it may curdle.) Once the seafood has cooked, stir the lemon juice through the fish and ladle the soup into the bread bowls. Garnish with chives and serve.

Clam Chowder

SERVES 6-8

255g/9oz butter
6 rashes of bacon, finely chopped
3 onions, finely chopped
1½ cups finely chopped celery
1 cup plain flour
4 cups milk
3 cups fish stock
500g/1lb potatoes, finely diced
1kg/2lb clam meat
salt and pepper
cream (optional), to serve
10 tablespoons chopped fresh parsley

Heat the butter in a saucepan and cook the bacon, onion and celery until tender.

Add the flour and cook for 2 minutes.

Add milk, fish stock and potatoes, cover and simmer for 10 minutes.

Add the clam meat and cook again for 10 minutes. Season to taste.

Serve in a deep plate with cream and parsley.

Mussel Soup

Serves 4

Place the water, carrot, cauliflower, capsicum, onion, saffron and coriander seeds in a large pot over high heat. Bring to the boil and add the vinegar.

Remove from the heat and allow to cool down. When cold, strain the vegetables from the cooking liquid.

In a cooking pot over medium heat, melt the butter then add the flour. Stir with a wooden spoon and cook gently for 2 minutes.

Add the broth slowly with a whisk and cook until slightly thickened and smooth in consistency.

Add the reserved vegetables, mussels and cream and bring to the boil. Add salt and pepper to taste. Garnish with parsley just before serving.

300mL/10fl oz water
1 small carrot, finely diced
55g/2oz cauliflower, divided into florets
½ red capsicum/pepper, finely diced
½ onion, finely diced
1 pinch saffron
10 coriander/cilantro seeds, cracked
45mL/1½ fl oz sherry vinegar
55g/2 oz butter
2 tablespoons plain flour
1kg/2 lbs mussels, cooked mariniéres style, reserving cooking broth.
2 tablespoons double cream
1 tablespoon parsley, finely chopped

Clam Bisque

Serves 4–6

500g/1 lb white fish fillets
3 cups milk
salt and pepper, to taste
1/8 teaspoon nutmeg
1 bay leaf
250g/8 oz jar mussels
2 tablespoons butter
1 medium-sized onion, finely chopped
2 stalks celery, finely cubed
3 tablespoons plain flour
1 tablespoon lemon juice
1 tablespoon finely chopped parsley or chives
1–2 tablespoons dry sherry
¼ cup cream

Cut the fish fillets into 2cm (¾ in) squares. Place in a saucepan with the milk, salt, pepper, nutmeg and bay leaf. Bring gently to the boil, then simmer slowly for 10 minutes. Stand covered for 10 minutes to infuse the flavours. Strain the milk from the fish and reserve. Keep the fish warm.

Drain the liquid from the mussels and rinse in cold water. Cut the mussels into 2 or 3 pieces.

Melt the butter in a large saucepan, add the onion and celery and cook gently for 10 minutes without browning. When soft, stir in the flour and cook for 1 minute while stirring.

Remove the saucepan from the heat and gradually stir in the reserved milk, stirring well after each addition until free from lumps. Return to the heat and stir until the mixture boils and thickens.

Add the lemon juice, chopped mussels, chopped parsley, sherry and cooked fish. Simmer slowly for 10 minutes. Stir in the cream and simmer for 5 minutes more. Serve in individual bowls, with croutons if desired.

Hot and Sour Seafood Soup

SERVES 6

4 red or golden eschallots, sliced
2 fresh green chillies, chopped
6 kaffir lime leaves
4 slices fresh ginger
8 cups fish, chicken or vegetable stock
255g/9oz boneless firm fish fillets, cut into chunks
12 medium raw prawns/shrimp, shelled and deveined
12 mussels, scrubbed and beards removed
115g/4oz oyster or straw mushrooms
3 tablespoons lime juice
2 tablespoons Thai fish sauce (nam pla)
fresh coriander/cilantro leaves
lime wedges

Place the eschallots, chillies, lime leaves, ginger and stock in a saucepan and bring to the boil over a high heat. Reduce the heat and simmer for 3 minutes.

Add the fish, prawns, mussels and mushrooms and cook for 3–5 minutes or until the fish and seafood are cooked. Discard any mussels that do not open after 5 minutes of cooking. Stir in the lime juice and fish sauce. To serve, ladle the soup into bowls, scatter with coriander leaves and accompany with lime wedges.

Cold Marinated Mussel Salad

Serves 4-6

Place the water, carrot, cauliflower, capsicum, onion, saffron and coriander seeds in a pot over high heat.

Bring to the boil and add the vinegar.

Remove from the heat straight away and allow to cool down. When cold, strain the vegetables and discard the cooking liquid.

In a large salad bowl, mix together the salad, tomatoes, olive oil, vegetables and mussels. Season with salt and pepper.

285mL/10fl oz water
1 small carrot, diced finely
55g/2oz cauliflower, broken into florets
½ red capsicum/pepper, diced finely
½ onion, diced finely
pinch saffron
10 coriander/cilantro seeds, cracked
45mL/1½ fl oz sherry vinegar
285g/10 oz cooked mussel meat (equivalent to approximately 1kg/2lb mussels in their shells, cooked mariniéres style and chilled)

SALAD
handful mesclun salad mix
cherry tomatoes, quartered
3 tablespoons virgin olive oil
salt and pepper

Seafood Paella Salad

SERVES 6

4 cups chicken stock
510g/18 oz uncooked large prawns/ shrimp
1 uncooked lobster tail (optional)
510g/18 oz mussels in shells, cleaned
2 tablespoons olive oil
1 onion, chopped
2 ham steaks, cut into 1cm (½ in) cubes
2 cups aborio rice
½ teaspoon ground turmeric
115g/4 oz fresh or frozen peas
1 red capsicum/pepper, diced

GARLIC DRESSING
½ cup olive oil
¼ cup white wine vinegar
3 tablespoons mayonnaise
2 cloves garlic, crushed
2 tablespoons chopped fresh parsley
freshly ground black pepper

Place the stock in a large saucepan and bring to the boil. Add the prawns and cook for 1–2 minutes or until the prawns change colour. Remove and set aside. Add lobster tail and cook for 5 minutes or until the lobster changes colour and is cooked. Remove and set aside. Add the mussels and cook until the shells open – discard any mussels that do not open after 5 minutes. Remove and set aside. Strain the stock and reserve. Peel and devein the prawns, leaving the tails intact.

Heat the oil in a large saucepan, add the onion and cook for 4–5 minutes or until soft. Add the ham, rice and turmeric and cook, stirring, for 2 minutes. Add the reserved stock and bring to the boil. Reduce the heat, cover and simmer for 15 minutes or until the liquid is absorbed and the rice is cooked and dry. Stir in the peas and capsicum and set aside to cool. Cover and refrigerate for at least 2 hours.

To make the dressing, place the oil, vinegar, mayonnaise, garlic, parsley and black pepper to taste in a food processor or blender and process to combine.

To serve, place the seafood and rice in a large salad bowl, spoon over the dressing and toss to combine

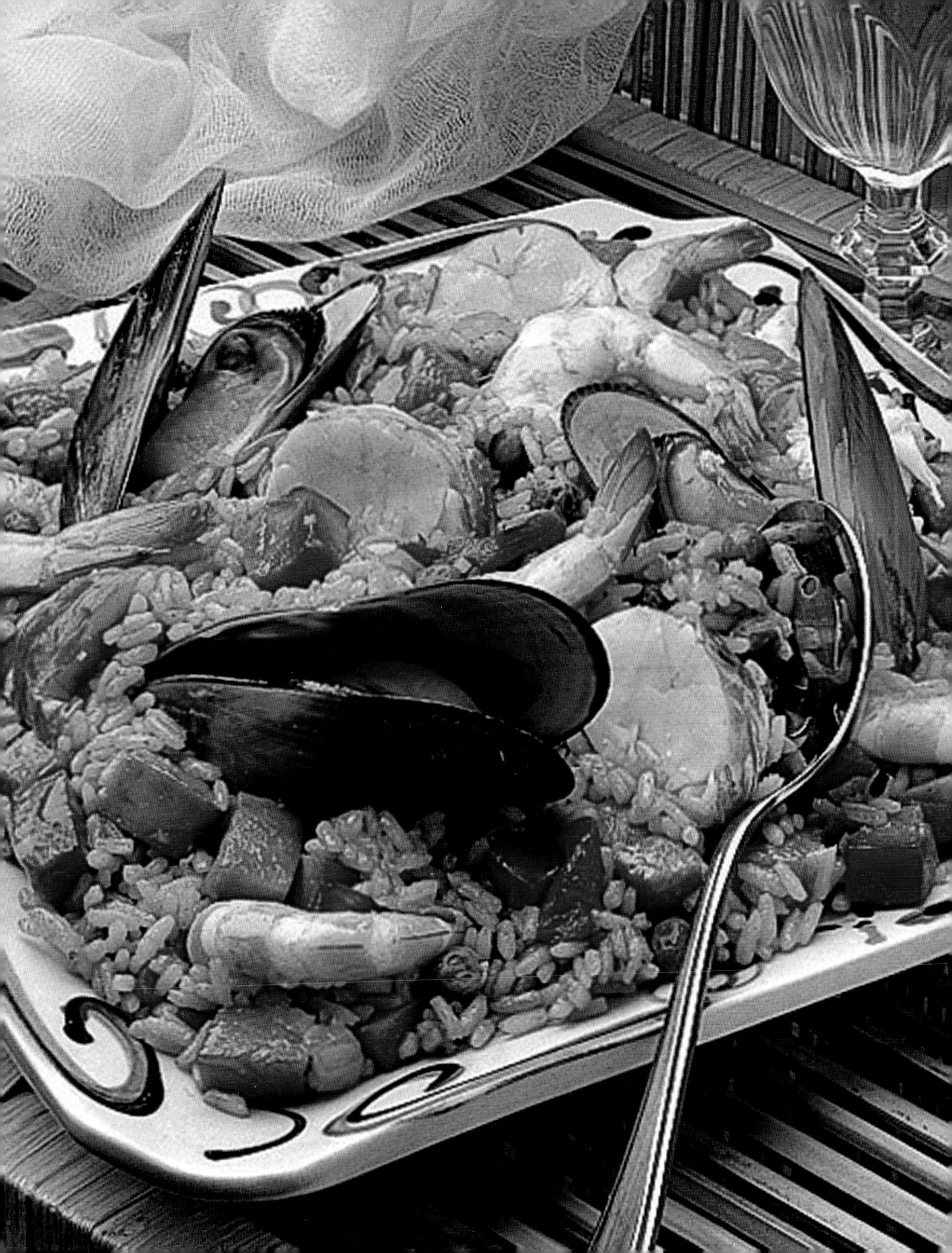

Witlof Speck Salad with Pipies and Mussels

SERVES 6-8

To prepare the marinated vegetables, place the ingredients together in a pot and boil for 2 minutes. Set aside to cool. When cold remove the liquid and keep the vegetables aside.

Mix all the other ingredients together with the marinated vegetables.

Refridgerate for 15 minutes until chilled.

400g/14 oz pipies cooked and removed from shells
400g/14 oz mussels cooked and removed from the shells
2 witlof, cut with leaves loose
4 slices of prosciutto, cooked under the grill and broken into small pieces
45mL/1½ fl oz virgin olive oil
1 tablespoon lemon juice
salt and pepper, to taste

MARINATED VEGETABLES
1 carrot, peeled and sliced
½ onion, sliced in half
½ stalk celery
15 coriander/cilantro seeds, cracked
salt and pepper
30mL/1fl oz sherry vinegar
1 cup water

Mixed Shellfish and Potato Salad

Serves 4

680g/1½ lb waxy potatoes, unpeeled
4 small cooked beetroot, diced
1 head fennel, finely sliced, plus feathery top, chopped
1kg/2 lb mussels
510g/18 oz clams
285mL/10fl oz dry white wine or apple cider
1 eschallot/French shallot finely chopped
4 spring onions/scallions, finely sliced
3 tablespoons chopped fresh parsley
DRESSING
5 tablespoons olive oil
1 tablespoons cider vinegar
1 teaspoon English mustard
salt and pepper

To make the dressing, whisk together the oil, vinegar, mustard and seasoning. Boil the potatoes in salted water for 15 minutes or until tender, then drain. Cool for 30 minutes, then peel and slice. Place in a bowl and toss with half the dressing. Toss the beetroot and fennel with the rest of the dressing.

Scrub the mussels and clams under cold running water, pulling away any beards from the mussels. Discard any shellfish that are open or damaged. Place the wine or cider and shallot in a large saucepan and bring to the boil. Simmer for 2 minutes, then add the shellfish. Cover and cook briskly for 3–5 minutes, shaking the pan often, or until the shellfish have opened. Discard any that remain closed. Reserve the pan juices, set aside a few mussels in their shells and shell the rest.

Boil the pan juices for 5 minutes or until reduced to 1–2 tablespoons. Strain over the potatoes. Add the shellfish, spring onions and parsley, then toss. Serve with the beetroot and fennel salad and garnish with the fennel tops and mussels in their shells.

Baked Mussels

Serves 4

Scrape the beard, and wash the mussels thoroughly. Place in a large saucepan with the shallots, thyme, parsley and bay leaf.

Sprinkle the salt over and then add the wine. Steam for 5 minutes or until the shells have opened. Open the mussels and discard the lids.

Divide the mussels in the remaining half shells into 4 ovenproof dishes. Make a herb butter by combining the butter, parsley, garlic and chives and place a generous portion on each mussel.

Bake at 190°C/370°F for approximately 3 minutes or until the butter has melted.

28 medium mussels
2 shallots/spring onions, finely chopped
1 sprig thyme
2 sprigs parsley
1 bay leaf
½ teaspoon salt
½ cup white wine
115g/4 oz butter or margarine, softened
1 tablespoon parsley, chopped
2 cloves garlic, crushed
1 tablespoon chives

Grilled Mussels

Serves 4

20 large fresh mussels
30g/1oz basil leaves
1 clove garlic, crushed
1 small red chilli, de-seeded and diced
½ teaspoon grated lemon rind
1 tablespoon pine nuts
1 tablespoon Parmesan cheese
1 tablespoon fresh breadcrumbs
salt and pepper
3–4 tablespoons extra virgin olive oil

Wash and scrub the mussels. Steam the mussels with just the water on their shells, for 4 minutes until they have just opened. Discard any which do not open. Immediately plunge the mussels into cold water and drain again.

Remove the mussels from the pan and carefully discard one half of each shell. Arrange the remaining mussels in 1 large dish or 4 individual gratin dishes.

In a blender or food processor combine the basil, garlic, chilli, lemon rind, pine nuts, Parmesan and half of the breadcrumbs. Pulse briefly to form a smooth paste and season to taste with salt and pepper.

Transfer the basil paste to a bowl and stir in the oil. Spoon a little of the paste over each mussel and finally top each one with a few more breadcrumbs. Cook under a preheated grill for 2–3 minutes until bubbling and golden. Serve immediately.

Clams with White Wine and Garlic

Serves 4

Wash the clams well. Leave them in cold water to which you have added a little salt for about an hour to get rid of any grit they may have in them.

Heat oil in a frying pan. Add the onion and garlic and sauté until golden brown. Add clams and cook over medium heat until the shells open. Add the flour and stir in well. Pour in the wine, add the paprika, bay leaf and some salt and pepper to taste. Continue cooking for a further 5 minutes.

Remove the bay leaf and serve the clams in the sauce. Half the fun is to eat the clam and then spoon up some sauce using the shell as a spoon.

680g/1½ lb medium to small clams
salt and pepper
45mL/1½ fl oz olive oil
1 small onion, peeled and finely chopped
3 cloves garlic, peeled and minced
1 tablespoon plain flour
100mL/31/2 fl oz dry white wine
pinch of paprika
1 bay leaf
salt and pepper to taste

Fried Vongole

SERVES 4

2 eggs, lightly beaten
salt and pepper
2 cups breadcrumbs
1 tablespoon dry mixed aromatic herbs
1kg/2 lb clams cleaned, cooked mariniéres style and removed from shell
1 cup vegetable oil, for frying
3 tablespoons tartare sauce
sliced lemon and salad leaves, to serve

Place the eggs in a bowl and season with a little salt and pepper.

Combine the breadcrumbs and herbs in a separate bowl.

Dip the clams in the egg mixture, then roll in breadcrumbs.

Heat oil in a frying pan and when hot, deep-fry the clams, until golden brown.

Drain on absorbent paper and serve immediately with tartare sauce.

Mussels with Tomatoes and Wine

Serves 4

For the sauce, heat the oil in a non-stick frying pan over a medium heat. Add the garlic and shallots. Cook, stirring, for 1–2 minutes. Add the salmon and the capsicum. Cook, stirring, for 3 minutes. Stir in the tomato paste. Cook for 3–4 minutes or until it becomes deep red and develops a rich aroma. Add the tomatoes. Cook, stirring, for 5 minutes or until the mixture starts to thicken. Stir in the parsley. Keep warm.

Meanwhile, place the mussels, shallot and wine in a large saucepan over a high heat. Cover. Bring to the boil then reduce the heat. Cook for 5 minutes or until the mussels open. Discard any mussels that do not open after 5 minutes of cooking.

Add the sauce to the mussels. Toss to combine.

To serve, divide the mixture among deep bowls. Scatter with chives. Accompany with crusty bread.

1kg/2 lb fresh mussels, scrubbed and beards removed
1 shallot/spring onion, chopped
1 cup dry white wine
chopped fresh chives

TOMATO AND SMOKED SALMON SAUCE
2 teaspoons olive oil
2 cloves garlic, crushed
2 shallots/spring onions, chopped
2–3 slices smoked salmon, sliced into thin strips
1 red capsicum/pepper, sliced
1 tablespoon tomato paste (no added salt)
400g/14 oz canned diced tomatoes (no added salt)
2 tablespoons chopped fresh parsley

Spaghettini with Baby Clams, Chilli and Garlic

Serves 4-6

400g/14 oz spaghettini
55mL/2fl oz olive oil
4 cloves garlic, sliced
4 red chillies, finely chopped
2 cups tomato, finely diced
680g/24 oz canned baby clams or fresh,cooked, if available
1/3 cup parsley, chopped
juice of 2 lemons
salt and freshly ground black pepper

Cook the spaghettini in boiling water with a little oil until al dente. Drain in a colander and rinse under cold water until cold. Set aside.

Heat half the oil and cook the garlic on a low heat until beginning to change colour. Add the chillies and tomato, and cook for a few minutes.

Add the clams, parsley, lemon juice, remaining oil, spaghettini and a little of the water used to cook the clams, and heat through for a further 5 minutes. Season with salt and black ground pepper to taste.

If using fresh clams, wash under running water, scraping the shells with a sharp knife or scourer. Place them in a large pan with a little water over a gentle heat until they open. Discard any that do not open.

Spaghetti Marinara

Serves 4

1 lb/500g spaghetti
2 teaspoons vegetable oil
2 teaspoons butter
2 onions, chopped
2 x 14oz/398mL canned tomatoes, undrained and mashed
2 tablespoons chopped fresh basil
¼ cup dry white wine
12 mussels, scrubbed and beards removed
12 scallops
4 oz/125g calamari/squid rings

Cook pasta in boiling water in a large saucepan following package directions. Drain, set aside and keep warm.

Heat oil and butter in a frying pan over a medium heat. Add onions and cook, stirring, for 4 minutes or until onions are golden.

Stir in tomatoes, basil and wine, bring to simmering and simmer for 8 minutes. Add mussels, scallops and prawns and cook for 2 minutes longer.

Add calamari (squid) and cook for 1 minute or until shellfish is cooked. Spoon shellfish mixture over hot pasta and serve immediately.

Mussels Mariniéres

Serves 3–4

1kg/2 lb mussels, cleaned
1 small onion, sliced
1 stalk celery, sliced
1 clove garlic, chopped
55mL/2fl oz water or white wine
pepper
1 tablespoon butter
1 tablespoon parsley, chopped

Place the mussels, onion, celery, garlic and water (or white wine) in a large saucepan.

Cook over medium heat until the mussels have opened, about 5 minutes. Stir frequently to ensure the mussels cook evenly.

Add pepper to taste. Stir in the butter and parsley just before serving.

Mussels Provençal

Serves 2

Place the oil, capsicum, tomatoes, garlic, celery and onion in a saucepan over medium heat. Cook for 4 minutes.

Add the mussels and white wine. Cook until the mussels are opened, stirring frequently.

Stir in the basil just before serving.

1 tablespoon olive oil
½ red capsicum/pepper, chopped
2 tomatoes, roughly chopped
1 clove garlic, chopped
1 stalk celery, sliced
1 onion, chopped
1kg/2 lb mussels, cleaned
45mL/1½fl oz white wine
1 tablespoon chopped basil

Spaghetti Vongole

Serves 3–4

285g/10 oz spaghetti
45mL/1½ fl oz virgin olive oil
1 onion, very finely chopped
2 cloves garlic, finely chopped
510g/18 oz clams, cleaned and sand removed
100mL/3⅓ fl oz white wine
salt and pepper
1 tablespoon fresh chopped oregano

Pre-cook the spaghetti in boiling water. Refresh in cold water, drain, mix in half the oil and set aside.

Heat the remaining oil in a large cooking pot over high heat. Add the onion, garlic and cook for 1 minute

Add the clams, white wine, salt and pepper.

When all the clams have opened, add the spaghetti and oregano. Cook for another 2 minutes and serve.

Spaghetti with Mussels

Serves 4

Pre-cook the spaghetti in water. Refresh in a cold water after cooking, drain, and toss with half the oil. Set aside.

Heat the remaining oil over a high heat in a large pot. Add the onion, garlic and tomatoes and cook for 10 minutes.

Add the mussels, chopped herbs, white wine and salt and pepper.

When the mussels start to open add the spaghetti.

Stir together until all the mussels have opened.

Serve with the Parmesan and parsely sprinkled on top.

225g/8 oz spaghetti
100mL/3½fl oz olive oil
1 onion, finely chopped
3 cloves garlic, finely chopped
4 vine ripened tomatoes, diced finely
510g/18oz mussels, cleaned
1 tablespoon fresh aromatic herbs (such as basil), chopped
100mL/3½ fl oz dry white wine
salt and pepper to taste
2 tablespoon grated Parmesan cheese
1 tablespoon chopped parsley

Seafood Paella

Serves 8

1 tablespoon olive oil
2 onions, chopped
2 cloves garlic, crushed
1 tablespoon fresh thyme leaves
2 teaspoons finely grated lemon rind
4 ripe tomatoes, chopped
2½ cups short-grain white rice
pinch saffron threads soaked in 2 cups water
5 cups chicken or fish stock
285g/10 oz fresh or frozen peas
2 red capsicums/peppers, chopped
1kg/2 lb mussels, scrubbed and beards removed
510g/18 oz firm white fish fillets, chopped
285g/10 oz peeled uncooked prawns/shrimp
225g/8 oz scallops
3 calamari/squid tubes, sliced
1 tablespoon chopped fresh parsley

Preheat the barbecue to a medium heat. Place a large paella or frying pan on the barbecue, add the oil and heat. Add the onions, garlic, thyme leaves and lemon rind and cook for 3 minutes or until the onion is soft.

Add the tomatoes and cook, stirring, for 4 minutes. Add the rice and cook, stirring, for 4 minutes longer or until the rice is translucent. Stir in the saffron mixture and stock and bring to a simmer. Simmer, stirring occasionally, for 30 minutes or until the rice has absorbed almost all of the liquid. Stir in the peas, capsicums and mussels and cook for 2 minutes. Add the fish, prawns and scallops and cook, stirring, for 2–3 minutes. Stir in calamari and parsley and cook, stirring, for 1–2 minutes longer or until the seafood is cooked.

Fried Mussels

Serves 4

2 eggs, lightly beaten
salt and pepper
2 cups breadcrumbs
1 tablespoon dry mixed aromatic herbs
1kg/2¼ lb black mussels cleaned, cooked mariniéres style and removed from the shell
1 cup vegetable oil, for frying
3 tablespoons tartare sauce
lemon wedges and salad, to serve

Place the eggs in a bowl and season with a little salt and pepper.

Combine the breadcrumbs and herbs in a separate bowl.

Dip the mussels in the egg mixture, then roll in breadcrumbs.

Heat oil in a frying pan until hot, deep-fry the mussels in hot oil, until golden brown.

Drain on absorbent paper and serve immediately with tartare sauce, lemon wedges and salad.

Chilli-Spiked Mussels in Spaghetti

Serves 4

340g/12 oz dried spaghetti
1kg/2¼ lb fresh mussels
2 tablespoon olive oil, plus 1 tablespoon extra for drizzling
2 shallots/spring onions, finely chopped
4 cloves garlic, chopped
145mL/5fl oz dry white wine
grated rind of 1 lemon
1 teaspoon dried chilli flakes
2 tablespoons chopped fresh parsley
black pepper, to taste

Cook the pasta according to the packet instructions, until tender but still firm to the bite, then drain well. Meanwhile, scrub the mussels under cold running water, pull away any beards and discard any mussels that are open or damaged.

Place the mussels in a large heavy-based saucepan, with just the water clinging to the shells. Steam mussels for 3–4 minutes over a high heat, shaking regularly, until the shells have opened. Discard any mussels that remain closed.

Heat 2 tablespoons of oil in a large saucepan and gently fry the shallots and garlic for 5 minutes or until softened. Add the wine and boil rapidly for 5–6 minutes, until the liquid has reduced by half. Add the mussels, lemon rind and chilli and heat for 2–3 minutes. Add the pasta to the mussels, then stir in the parsley and season with black pepper. Gently toss over heat and drizzle remaining oil over.

Belgian-Style Mussels

Serves 4

2kg/4 lb mussels in their shells
30g/1 oz butter
1 tablespoon vegetable oil
4 shallots/spring onion or 1 onion, chopped
2 stalks celery, chopped, plus any leaves
145mL/5fl oz dry white wine
black pepper
145mL/5fl oz thickened or double cream
4 tablespoons chopped fresh flat-leaf Italian parsley

Scrub the mussels under cold running water, then pull away any beards and discard any mussels that are open or damaged. Heat the butter and oil in a very large saucepan, then add the shallots or onion and celery and cook for 2–3 minutes, until the shallots are translucent.

Stir in the wine and plenty of pepper and bring to the boil. Add the mussels, cover and cook over a high heat, shaking the pan occasionally, for 4–5 minutes, until the mussels have opened. Using a slotted spoon, remove mussels from the pan and keep warm in a bowl, discarding any that remain closed.

Roughly chop the celery leaves, reserving a few for garnish. Add chopped leaves, cream and parsley to the cooking juices and season again if necessary. Bring to the boil, then spoon sauce over the mussels. Garnish with celery leaves.

Mussel Shooters

SERVES 6

18 Mussels, cooked mariniéres style, removed from the shell
BLOODY MARY MIX
200mL/7fl oz tomato juice
60mL/2fl oz vodka
a few drops of Worcestershire sauce
a few drops of Tabasco sauce
celery salt and pepper
sliced lemon and baby dill pickles, to garnish

Combine all the bloody Mary ingredients and stir until combined. Refrigerate for 2–3 hours.

Take 6 shooter glasses and add 3 mussels to each glass. Top the glasses with Bloody Mary mix, garnish with lemon and dill pickles, and serve immediately.

Escargot Mussels

Serves 4

Remove the extra half shell and keep the mussel in one shell.

To make garlic butter, combine all the ingredients in a bowl and mix well.

Top the half shell mussel with garlic butter.

Grill the mussels until sizzling, sprinkle with chives and serve with salad and bread

1kg/2¼ lb mussels, cooked mariniéres style.
GARLIC BUTTER
510g/18oz softened butter
2 cloves garlic, minced
1 tablespoon chopped fresh parsely
30mL/1fl oz brandy
salt and pepper
chopped chives
salad and bread, to serve

Mussels in Pernod Cream

Serves 4

2kg/4½ lb mussels
¾ cup dry white wine
1 tablespoon chopped parsley
a small bouquet garni (see glossary)
90g/3 oz butter
2 medium onions, finely chopped
1 clove garlic, chopped
¾ cup hot milk
2 egg yolks
¾ cup cream
3 tablespoons Pernod (or lemon juice)
freshly ground pepper
2 tablespoons chopped parsley
8 slices French bread

Clean the mussels and place in a large pan with the wine, parsley, and bouquet garni. Cover and cook for about 5 minutes until the mussels are opened. Discard any unopened mussels. Strain the resulting broth through a fine sieve. Remove the top shell from the mussels and discard. Keep the mussels warm.

Heat the butter in a pan and sauté the onions and garlic gently until pale golden and soft. Add the strained mussel broth and 2 cups of boiling water plus the milk. Simmer for 5 minutes.

Beat the egg yolks with the cream and Pernod or lemon juice. Stir in a little of the hot soup then return this mixture to the pan. Reheat gently, stirring all the time. Season with pepper. Place the mussels in 4 large warm soup plates, pour the hot sauce over and sprinkle with parsley.

Meanwhile, fry the bread in the oil or butter until golden on both sides. Serve with the mussels.

Clams in White Wine Sauce

Serves 4-6

7 tablespoons olive oil
2 tablespoons minced onion
4 cloves garlic, minced
2 dozen small clams, scrubbed, at room temperature
1 tablespoon flour
1 tablespoon paprika
2 tablespoons minced parsley
1 cup semi-sweet white wine
1 bay leaf
1 dried red chilli pepper, cut into 3 pieces, seeds removed
freshly ground pepper
salt

Heat the oil in a large, shallow frying pan. Sauté the onion and garlic until the onion is wilted. Add the clams and cook, uncovered, over medium-high heat until they open. (If some open much sooner than others, remove them so they do not toughen. Return to the pan when all have opened.)

Sprinkle in the flour and stir, then add the paprika, parsley, wine, bay leaf, chilli, pepper, and salt, if necessary (the liquid the clams release may be salty). Continue cooking and stirring for another 5 minutes. Serve in the cooking dish if possible, and let everyone help themselves.

Lemon and Garlic Steamed Mussels

Serves 2

2 dozen mussels, small or medium-sized
3 tablespoons olive oil
2 tablespoons fresh lemon juice
2 cloves garlic, minced

Place the mussels in a frying pan without water. Cover and cook over medium heat, removing the mussels to a warm platter as they open. Discard any that do not open.

Reduce liquid in the frying pan to about 2 or 3 tablespoons, then return the mussels to the pan. Sprinkle with the oil, lemon juice and garlic and heat for 1 minute. Serve immediately, with plenty of good bread for dunking.

Mussels Riviera

SERVES 4

Heat the oil, add the onion, garlic, tomatoes and capsicum (bell pepper) in a saucepan and cook slowly for 5 minutes.

Add white wine and herbs, season with salt, pepper and paprika. Cook slowly for 30 minutes until the mixture reaches a paste consistency.

Using a spoon, cover the mussels with the paste, top up with Parmesan. Place under the grill and heat until the Parmesan has lightly browned. Serve with foccacia bread.

1kg/2 lb mussels, mariniéres style, removed in half shell

RIVIERA MIX

olive oil

1 onion, finely chopped

2 garlic cloves, chopped

4 tomatoes, finely chopped

½ red capsicum/pepper, chopped finely

200mL/7fl oz white wine

2 tablespoons rosemary, thyme and basil mix, dry or freshly chopped

salt, pepper and paprika

1 tablespoon grated Parmesan cheese

Mussel Risotto

Serves 4

200mL/7 oz olive oil
1 onion, finely chopped
2 cloves garlic, finely chopped
1 red capsicum/pepper, diced
285g/10 oz arborio rice
2¼ cups dry white wine
1kg/2 lb mussels, cleaned
1 tablespoon chopped fresh aromatic herbs (thyme, rosemary, marjoram)
2 tablespoons grated Parmesan cheese
sliced chives, to serve

Place the oil in a pot over medium heat.

Add the onion, garlic and capsicum and cook for 2 minutes.

Add rice and half the wine. Stir with a wooden spatula and cook until the rice is almost dry.

Add mussels and the other half of the wine.

Add the herbs and cook until the rice and mussels are cooked. Replace the lid and stir frequently to avoid the rice sticking to the pot.

Serve sprinkled with grated Parmesan and sliced chives.

Spinach Mornay Mussels

Serves 3-4

1kg/2 lb mussels, cleaned
2 tablespoons butter
3 tablespoons plain flour
400mL/14fl oz milk
salt, pepper and nutmeg
200g/7oz grated cheddar
55g/2oz Parmesan cheese
lemon wedges and mixed leaf salad to serve

Cook the mussels mariniéres style and remove 1 shell from each mussel.

Melt the butter slowly in a pot. Do not allow the butter to burn.

Add the flour and mix until very smooth, using a wooden spatula. Remove from the heat.

Add the milk with a whisk and return to the heat. Stir with the whisk until boiling. Reduce the heat and cook slowly for 5 minutes. Season with salt, pepper and nutmeg.

Add the cheeses. Cook for another 5 minutes on low heat, until the cheese is completely melted.

Top up the half-shell mussels with the mornay sauce and heat under the grill until golden brown. Serve with lemon wedges and mixed leaf salad.

Blue Cheese Mussels

Serves 3–4

2 tablespoons olive oil
1 onion, chopped
1 stalk celery, sliced
½ stalk of leek, rinsed and sliced
1kg/2 lb mussels, cleaned
100mL/3½ fl oz white wine
55g/2oz blue cheese, broken into small pieces
1 handful of fresh spinach leaves
juice of 1 lemon
30g/1 oz butter
1 tablespoon chopped parsley

Place the oil, onion, celery and leek in a pot and cook for 2 minutes, stirring frequently.

Add the mussels, white wine, blue cheese, spinach, lemon juice and cook until the mussels have opened.

Add the butter and parsley, stir and serve.

Chinese-Style Mussels

SERVES 4

Mix all the sauce ingredients together

Place the sesame oil, mussels and water in a pot and cook until the mussels start to open.

Add the sauce and cook until all the mussels are open.

Add cornflour mixture and stir until the sauce thickens. This should take around 1 minute.

Add the coriander and shallots. Serve mussels with rice or noodles.

1 tablespoon sesame oil
1kg/2 lb mussels cleaned
55mL/2fl oz water
1 tablespoon cornflour or arrowroot mix with 2 tablespoons cold water
1 tablespoon fresh coriander/cilantro, chopped
3 shallots/spring onions, finely chopped

SAUCE

100mL/3½ fl oz oyster sauce
1 tablespoon fresh chopped ginger
1 red chilli, sliced
1 clove garlic, chopped
1 tablespoon white vinegar
1 tablespoon soy sauce
1 pinch of Chinese five spice

Curry Mussels

Serves 2

2 tablespoons olive oil
1 small onion, chopped
1 stalk celery, sliced
1 clove garlic, chopped
2 tablespoon yellow curry paste
2 cardamom pods, crushed
1 pinch ground cumin
1kg/2 lb mussels, cleaned
55mL/2fl oz coconut cream
1 tablespoon fresh chopped coriander/cilantro

Place oil, onion, celery, garlic, curry paste, cardamom and cumin in a pot and cook over a low heat for 5 minutes, stirring frequently.

Add the mussels and coconut cream and cook over high heat.

Cook until all the mussels have opened, stirring every minute to the ensure mussels are cooked evenly.

Add the coriander, stir and serve. Add chopped chilli if you like it extra spicy.

Laksa

Serves 4

Place the oil, onion, garlic and laksa paste in a large pot and cook for 3–5 minutes over medium heat.

Add the chicken stock and lemon grass. Add mussels and cook until the mussels start to open.

Add the coconut cream, rice noodles and lime leaf. Cook for a further 4 minutes.

Serve when all the mussels have opened, sprinkled with sliced shallots.

45mL/1½ fl oz peanut oil or vegetable oil
1 onion, finely chopped
3 cloves garlic, chopped
1 tablespoon laksa paste
400mL/14fl oz chicken stock
1 stick lemon grass, chopped
510g/18 oz mussels, cleaned
225mL/8fl oz coconut cream
145g/5 oz rice noodles
1 lime leaf, finely chopped
sliced shallots, to serve

Mussels Tin Tin

Serves 2

55mL/2fl oz white wine
1 red chilli, sliced
1 stalk lemon grass, crushed
1 tablespoon fresh chopped ginger
1 clove garlic, chopped
1 tablespoon peanut oil
1kg/2 lb mussels, cleaned
100mL/3½ fl oz coconut cream
1 tablespoon fresh coriander/cilantro, chopped

Place the white wine, chilli, lemon grass, ginger and garlic in a pot and set aside to allow the flavours to infuse together for 15 minutes.

In a separate pot, gently heat the oil and mussels. Add to the white wine mixture.

Add coconut cream and cook until the mussels have opened, stirring frequently.

Stir in the coriander and serve

Spanish Marinated Mussels

Serves 4

1kg/2 lb mussels, cooked mariniéres style and removed from the shell
1 hard-boiled egg (white only), chopped finely
2 tablespoons baby capers
2 tablespoons fresh aromatic herbs, (thyme, rosemary, marjoram) chopped
2 vine-ripened tomatoes, finely chopped
145mL/5fl oz Spanish virgin olive oil
1 tablespoon Dijon mustard
30mL/1fl oz sherry vinegar
1 tablespoon fresh basil, roughly chopped
salt and pepper

Combine all the ingredients and marinate in the refrigerator for 2 hours.

Serve with salad or as part of a sharing or tapas menu.

Pipies in Black Beans

Serves 4

1 tablespoon sesame oil

1 kg/2 lb pipies cleaned and sand removed

55mL/2fl oz water

1 tablespoon corn flour, mixed with 2 tablespoons water

1 tablespoon fresh coriander/ cilantro, chopped

3 shallots/spsring onions, finely sliced

BLACK BEAN SAUCE

4 tablespoons fermented black beans (salted black beans)

1 tablespoon fresh chopped ginger

1 chopped red chilli

2 garlic cloves chopped

1 tablespoon white vinegar

2 tablespoons soy sauce

1 pinch Chinese five spice

1 teaspoon sugar

2 tablespoons vegetable oil

To make the sauce, rinse the fermented black beans thoroughly and then mince (not rinsing the beans will make the sauce too salty). Mix all the sauce ingredients, set aside for 15 minutes.

On high heat and in a large pot, put the sesame oil, pipies and water and cook until the pipies start to open.

Add the sauce mix and cook until all the pipies have opened.

Add the corn flour and stir until the sauce has thickened, around 1 minute on high heat.

Add the coriander and spring onions.

Serve with rice or noodles.

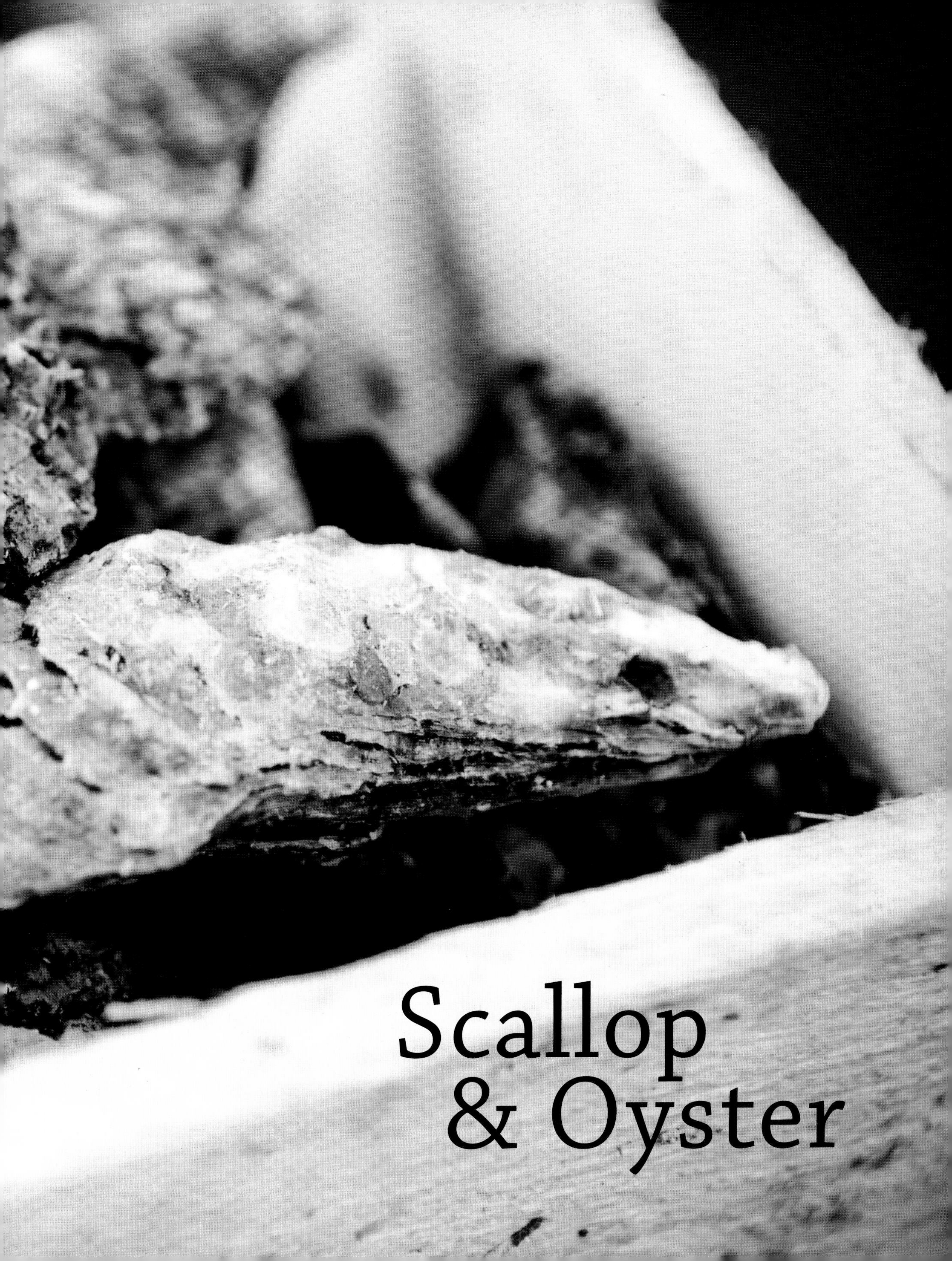

Scallop & Oyster

Introduction

Scallops are one of the most delectable foodstuffs to come from the sea. Scallops are so rich, sweet and tender that a little goes a long way. Beware, however, that some unscrupulous markets may try to palm off imposter seafood as scallops. Learn how to spot a true scallop, discover its history, and try some new recipes using this seafood treat.

Types of Scallops

The scallop is a bivalve mollusk of the family Pectinidae. There are many varieties of scallop, ranging from the tiny, tender bay scallop to the larger, less tender deep sea scallop. The entire scallop within the shell is edible, but it is the white adductor muscle which hinges the two shells that is most commonly sold.

Oysters

Oysters are a very healthy food, and some claim they have aphrodisiac powers! They are easily digested, rich in vitamins and minerals. Oysters are highly adaptable and are currently being grown successfully in many locations.

Oysters are classified as shellfish, being covered with a shell, or invertebrates, having no backbone. They are further classified as mollusks, being of soft structure either partially or wholly enclosed in a hard shell that is largely of mineral composition.

Research shows that oysters are low in cholesterol and high in omega-3 fats, calcium, iron, zinc, copper and protein. All shellfish have some carbohydrate. Oysters contain 3–5 percent. Oysters also contain a somewhat higher percentage of calcium than other fish and meats, which are notably low in calcium. Oysters, clams and lobster contain more iodine than any other seafood. Few foods can compare to oysters in terms of their nutritional value.

Oysters may be purchased live in the shell, fresh or frozen shucked (removed from the shell), or canned. When alive, they have a tightly closed shell.

Scallop Preparation

Like all shellfish, scallops deteriorate quickly once out of the water, so they are usually sold shucked (shelled). When you buy them, check to make sure they have a sweet odour and a moist sheen. Scallops range in colour from a light beige to a creamy pink. Beware of those that are stark white as they've likely been soaked in water to increase their weight for sale. Though the entire scallop, including the corals (roe), can be eaten, most scallops consist of the adductor muscle that hinges the two shells together.

Refrigerate fresh scallops immediately and use them within a day or two. Frozen scallops are an excellent option, as they are widely available year-round. If you are catching your own scallops, put them on ice immediately, as the cold causes them to open up. In contrast, warm scallops will demonstrate quite clearly the meaning of the expression 'to clam up'!

Opening Scallop Shells

Step 1: With the dark side of the scallop up and the hinge facing away from you, insert a knife blade or sharpened spoon between the top and bottom shells, inserting, from the right. Cut away the muscle at its attachment to the top shell. Remove the top shell and discard.

Step 2: Remove the dark innards by gently scraping from hinge to front with a spoon or scallop knife. The innards will peel cleanly from the muscle if you carefully scrape over the muscle from hinge to front, pinching the innards against the knife or spoon with your thumb as you pass over the cut surface of the muscle.

Step 3: Now simply scrape the scallop from the bottom shell. Some people prefer to leave the muscle attached.

Oyster Preparation

Fresh oysters are available year-round, although for serving raw, they're at their best during autumn and winter. Buy oysters from places with a rapid turn-over to insure freshness, and select only those with tightly closed shells (or that snap shut when tapped).

Cover live oysters with a damp towel and refrigerate, larger shells down, for up to 3 days. You can also purchase shucked (shelled) oysters. Look for plump meat with uniform size, good colour and fresh smell, packed in clear (not cloudy) oyster liquor. Use shucked oysters within 2 days. Oysters are also available canned in water or oyster liquor, frozen and smoked.

If you use technique rather than strength, oysters are easy to open. Hold the unopened oyster in a garden glove or tea towel to protect your hand from the rough shell. Open it with an oyster knife held in the other hand.

Step 1: Hold the oyster with the deep cut down and insert the tip of the oyster knife into the hinge. Twist to open the shell. Do not open oyster by attempting to insert the oyster knife into the front lip of the shell.

Step 2: Slide the oyster knife inside the upper shell to cut the muscle that attaches it to the shell. To serve, discard the upper part of shell, cut the muscle under the bottom half, then replace oyster into half shell.

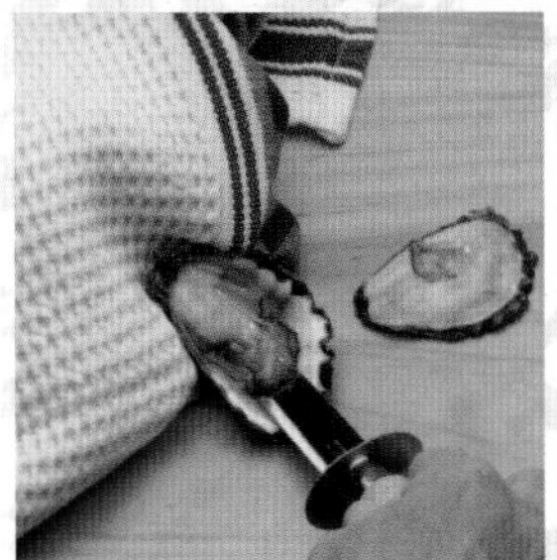

Oysters in Tempura Batter

SERVES 4

20 oysters

DIPPING SAUCE

4 tablespoons/60mL dark soy sauce

4 tablespoons/60mL water

juice of 1 lime

sunflower oil for deep frying

TEMPURA BATTER

½ cup cornstarch

½ cup plain/all-purpose flour

small pinch salt

4 teaspoons toasted sesame seeds

¾ cup ice cold soda water

sliced shallot/spring onion

lime wedges to serve

Open all the oysters and pour off the liquid. Carefully cut the meat out of the deeper shells and retain the shells for serving.

Mix together the ingredients for the dipping sauce and pour into 4 dipping saucers.

Heat oil in a deep fryer or frying pan to 375°F/190°C.

Make the batter by sifting the cornstarch, flour and salt into a mixing bowl. Stir in the sesame seeds then stir in the ice cold soda water until just mixed. Add a little more water if it seems too thick. The batter should be very thin and almost transparent.

Dip the oysters, one at a time. Drop into the hot oil and fry for a minute until crisp and golden. Lift out and drain on paper towels.

Return the oysters to their shells and arrange on plates, or place in ceramic Chinese soup spoons. Serve topped with shallot, lime wedges and dipping sauce.

Grilled Oysters with Champagne and Cream

Serves 4

12 fresh oysters in their shells
3 tablespoons/45mL champagne, dry sparkling wine or dry vermouth
2 tablespoons/25mL butter
2 tablespoons/25mL heavy or whipping cream
black pepper
1½ cups baby spinach

Open oyster shells and scoop out each oyster with a teaspoon, straining any juices into a small saucepan. Remove and discard the muscle from the 12 rounded half shells, then wash and dry the shells. Place in a flameproof dish lined with crumpled foil so that the shells sit level.

Bring the oyster juices to a simmer and poach the oysters for 30–60 seconds, until just firm. Remove from the pan. Add the champagne to the pan and boil for 2 minutes to reduce. Remove from the heat and whisk in the butter, then the cream. Season with pepper.

Preheat the grill to high. Cook the spinach in a saucepan for 2–3 minutes, until wilted. Squeeze out the excess liquid and divide between the shells. Top with an oyster and spoon over a little sauce. Cook close to the grill for 1 minute or until heated through.

Poached Scallops with Ginger and Shallots

Serves 4

1 lb/500g fresh scallops
4 shallots/spring onions
1 medium carrot
4 sprigs flatleaf parsley
¾ cup water
¼ cup lemon juice
1 teaspoon soy sauce
2 teaspoons honey
2 teaspoons grated fresh ginger

Remove any dark membrane from the scallops, leaving coral attached. Rinse well.

Wash and peel shallots and carrot, cut into julienne strips. Pluck the parsley leaves from the stalks and rinse.

Heat water, lemon juice, soy sauce, honey and ginger to simmering point. Add the scallops, julienne strips and parsley and poach for 3–4 minutes. Do not overcook.

Remove to individual scallop shells or entrée dishes with a slotted spoon. Strain the poaching liquid, return to the saucepan and reduce over high heat to intensify the flavour. Spoon over the scallops and serve immediately.

Oysters Acapulco

Makes 24 oysters

CORIANDER PESTO
½ cup coriander/cilantro leaves
2 tablespoons pine nuts, toasted
1 clove garlic, roughly chopped
2 tablespoons Parmesan cheese, grated
2 tablespoons pecorino cheese, grated
¼ cup olive oil
salt and freshly ground black pepper
OYSTERS
24 oysters on the half shell
rock salt (optional)
½ cup finely diced red capsicum/pepper
½ cup crumbled Cacique or feta cheese

Heat grill. If grilling oysters, make a bed of rock salt in 2 baking pans and arrange the oysters in them. (If barbecueing, the oysters will go directly on the grill.)

Top each oyster with coriander pesto, diced capsicum and crumbled Cacique or feta cheese. Cook under grill until cheese has lightly browned.

Coriander Pesto

Place the coriander, pine nuts, garlic and cheeses in a food processor, and process, until a paste forms. With the motor still running, add oil in a steady stream, until well combined.

Season with salt and pepper, to taste. Store in fridge, with a little olive oil over top, to prevent coriander turning brown.

Tip: Mussels or clams can also be used in this recipe.

Oysters Greta Garbo

Serves 6 (entrée)

3 dozen oysters in shells
juice of ½ lime or lemon
6 slices smoked salmon, cut into fine strips
1 cup sour cream
2 tablespoons fresh chives, chopped, for garnish
red caviar for garnish
crushed ice for serving

Sprinkle the oysters with lime or lemon juice and top with smoked salmon.

Put a dollop of the sour cream onto each oyster.

Garnish with chives and red caviar.

Serve on a bed of ice with a slice of lime.

Oysters Kilpatrick

Serves 2–4 (entrée)

24 oysters on the shell
1 teaspoon Worcestershire sauce
1 cup cream
pepper and salt
8 oz/250g bacon strips, finely chopped
fine breadcrumbs

Remove oysters from shells and put aside. Put shells on a baking sheet and heat in a moderate oven. Mix Worcestershire sauce and cream. When shells are hot, return oysters to shells. Use tongs to handle the shells, as they get very hot. Add a little of the cream mixture to each shell and sprinkle with pepper and salt.

Top each oyster with chopped bacon and fine breadcrumbs. Place baking sheet under a hot grill and grill until bacon is crisp but not burnt and oysters are warmed through.

Oysters Kilpatrick are very tasty served with a bowl of hot puréed spinach and thin slices of buttered brown or rye bread.

Hot Oysters and Leeks

Serves 4

20–24 large oysters in the half shell
coarse sea salt
1 small leek, washed and finely sliced
2 tablespoons butter
salt, pepper and a pinch of sugar
squeeze of lemon juice
½ cup dry white wine
pinch of saffron threads or curry powder
½ cup cream
1 egg yolk
salt and white pepper
lime wedges to serve

Remove the oysters from their shells and keep chilled. Wash the shells and arrange in 4 individual gratin dishes, on a bed of coarse sea salt to keep them level.

Wash leek and slice it finely. Melt butter in a pan and toss the leek in the hot butter. Season with salt, freshly ground pepper and sugar, cover tightly and cook gently until tender. Season with lemon juice.

Boil the wine with the saffron or curry powder over a moderate heat until reduced by half. In a small bowl combine the cream with the egg yolk and whisk. Whisk in the hot wine mixture and return to gentle heat to thicken slightly, whisking all the time. Do not let it boil. Add salt and white pepper to taste and remove from heat.

Arrange the cooked leeks in the oyster shells and place oysters on top. Coat each oyster with the sauce and place under a preheated hot grill for a minute or so to glaze. Serve immediately.

Steamed Scallops with Black Beans and Garlic

Serves 4

12 large scallops (or 24 small scallops)
1 tablespoon dry sherry
1 tablespoon Chinese salted black beans
1 teaspoon freshly crushed garlic
3 teaspoons soy sauce
¼ teaspoon salt
pinch cracked black peppercorns
½ teaspoon sugar
1 teaspoon oil
1 teaspoon cornstarch
1 tablespoon sesame oil
1 shallot/spring onion (green part only),cut into fine slices
12 coriander/cilantro leaves
½ hot chilli, seeded and cut into 5mm/¼ ins diamond shapes

Use the 12 scallop shells for cooking and to serve. Mix scallops with the sherry, and then place one scallop in each shell. Set aside.

Soak black beans in enough cold water to cover for 15 minutes, then rinse, dry on paper towels, and mince. Combine beans, garlic, soy sauce, salt, pepper, sugar, oil and cornstarch. Distribute mixture evenly over each of the scallops, and trickle the sesame oil over each scallop.

Half fill a large pan with water and bring to a vigorous boil. Place a steaming rack large enough to hold all the scallops over the boiling water and place scallops in steamer rack. Cover tightly, and steam for 5 minutes. Remove, sprinkle with shallot, and garnish each scallop with one coriander leaf and a chilli diamond before serving.

Oysters Bloody Mary

Makes 6 oysters

Combine the ingredients and spread evenly over the opened oysters. Chill for 5–10 minutes. Serve with bread and butter, or hot buttered toast, with extra lime wedges and pepper.

Note: If liked, the oysters can also be grilled before serving.

splash of vodka
dash of Tabasco sauce
grind of black pepper
squeeze of fresh lime
flesh of 2 fresh tomatoes, chopped (no pulp or seeds)
½–1 teaspoon wholegrain mustard (optional)
lime and pepper for serving
6 scrubbed oysters, opened

Creamy Oyster Bisque

Serves 4

20 fresh oysters, shucked, or 1 jar drained, liquid reserved
low-salt fish or vegetable stock
½ cup white wine
1 small white onion or ½ leek, diced
1 stalk celery, diced
2 cups diced peeled potato
1 tablespoon chopped fresh thyme or 1 teaspoon dried thyme
½ cup low-fat milk
freshly ground black pepper
sprigs watercress or fresh parsley, to serve (optional)

Measure liquid from oysters. Add stock to make up to 1 cup.

Heat 2 tablespoons of the wine in a large saucepan over a low heat. Add onion and celery. Cook, stirring, for 4–5 minutes or until onion is transparent. Add potato and thyme. Stir in stock mixture and remaining wine. Bring to boil and simmer for 10–15 minutes or until potatoes are soft and most of the liquid is absorbed. Cool slightly.

Transfer mixture to a food processor or blender. Add half the oysters, the milk and black pepper to taste. Purée. Return mixture to a clean saucepan. Bring to the boil. Remove soup from heat and stir in remaining oysters.

To serve, ladle soup into warm bowls and top with watercress or parsley sprigs, if desired.

Hot and Sour Scallop Soup

Serves 4

Place chicken stock, mushrooms and bamboo shoots in saucepan. Bring to the boil, reduce heat and simmer 5 minutes. Rinse scallops under cold running water. Add scallops, soy sauce and pepper.

Bring to the boil. Mix the cornstarch with warm water. Add cornstarch mixture and stir a few seconds until thickened. Stir briskly with a chopstick and gradually pour in egg. Remove from heat. Stir in vinegar and sprinkle with shallots. Serve immediately.

4 cups salt reduced chicken stock
1 cup mushrooms, thinly sliced
¼ cup bamboo shoots, sliced
½ lb/250g scallops, sliced ¼ ins/5mm thick
1 teaspoon soy sauce
¼ teaspoon white pepper
2 tablespoons cornstarch
3 tablespoons warm water
1 egg, beaten
3 tablespoons rice vinegar (2 tablespoons white wine vinegar may be substituted)
⅓ cup thinly sliced shallots/spring onions

Scallop and Watercress Salad

Serves 4

10 fresh scallops
3 cups watercress, discard woody stems, select tender tips only
1 cup water chestnuts, halved
½ cup cherry tomatoes
½ cup walnut halves
1 cup bean sprouts, topped and tailed
DRESSING
⅔ cup walnut oil or olive oil
2 tablespoons red wine vinegar
2 small cloves garlic, minced
salt
white pepper

Mix the dressing ingredients together in a screw top jar and shake well.

Place the scallops on a plate suitable for steaming. Sprinkle scallops with a little of the dressing and steam gently over boiling water for 6 minutes.

Wash and dry the watercress, and snap into 5 ins/12cm sections. In a serving bowl, combine the watercress, water chestnuts, cherry tomatoes, walnuts and bean sprouts. Pour on the dressing and toss through the salad. Gently mix in the scallops.

Seared Scallop Salad

Serves 4

To make dressing, place mayonnaise, olive oil, vinegar and mustard in a bowl, mix to combine and set aside.

Heat sesame oil in a frying pan over a high heat, add garlic and scallops and cook, stirring, for 1 minute or until scallops just turn opaque. Remove scallop mixture from pan and set aside. Add bacon to pan and cook, stirring, for 4 minutes or until crisp. Remove bacon from pan and drain on paper towels.

Place lettuce leaves in a large salad bowl, add dressing and toss to coat. Add bacon, croutons and shavings of Parmesan cheese and toss to combine. Spoon scallop mixture over salad and serve.

2 teaspoons sesame oil
2 cloves garlic, crushed
12oz/375g scallops, cleaned
4 strips bacon, chopped
1 head romaine lettuce, leaves separated
1 cup croutons
fresh Parmesan cheese

MUSTARD DRESSING
3 tablespoons mayonnaise
1 tablespoon olive oil
1 tablespoon vinegar
2 teaspoons Dijon mustard

Warm Seafood Salad

SERVES 8

6 cups assorted salad leaves
2 or 3 yellow teardrop tomatoes
1 dozen cherry tomatoes, halved
2 avocados, pitted, peeled and sliced
1¼ cups snow peas/mange tout trimmed and blanched
8–10 asparagus spears, cut into 2in/5cm pieces, blanched
3 calamari/squid tubes
2 tablespoons butter
9oz/250g scallops
16 raw medium prawns/shrimp, shelled and deveined, tails left intact
7oz/200g thickly sliced smoked trout or smoked salmon

ORIENTAL DRESSING

1 tablespoon rice vinegar
1 tablespoon fish sauce
2 tablespoons sweet chilli sauce
1 tablespoon fresh basil, shredded
1 tablespoon lemon juice
¼ cup water

Arrange salad leaves, teardrop tomatoes and cherry tomatoes, avocados, snow peas and asparagus on a large serving platter.

To make dressing, place vinegar, fish sauce, chilli sauce, basil, lemon juice and water in a small bowl and whisk to combine.

Cut calamari tubes lengthwise, and open out flat. Using a sharp knife, cut parallel lines down the length of the calamari, taking care not to cut right through the flesh. Make more cuts in the opposite direction to form a diamond pattern. Cut each piece into 2 ins/5cm squares.

Melt butter in a large frying pan, add scallops and prawns and stir-fry for 3 minutes. Add calamari pieces and stir-fry for 1 minute longer. Arrange cooked seafood and smoked trout or smoked salmon on salad and drizzle with dressing.

Ginger Scallop Stir-Fry

Serves 4

2 tablespoons fresh lime juice
2 tablespoons rice wine
1 clove garlic, crushed
8oz/250g scallops
1 tablespoon sesame oil
2 teaspoons fresh ginger, finely grated
4 shallots/spring onions, cut diagonally into ½ ins/1cm lengths
1¼ cups button mushrooms, sliced
½ red capsicum/pepper, diced
2 teaspoons soy sauce
pepper
1 teaspoon cornstarch
2 tablespoons water
steamed white rice and lime wedges, to serve

Combine the lime juice with the rice wine and crushed garlic. Marinate the scallops for 15 minutes. Set aside.

Heat the sesame oil in a hot wok or large skillet until almost smoking. Add the ginger, shallots, mushrooms and capsicum. Stir-fry for about 3 minutes, until the ginger has become fragrant.

Add the scallops and marinade. Continue stir-frying for another 3 minutes, until scallops have become opaque. Add the soy sauce and mix thoroughly. Add pepper to taste.

Mix the cornstarch and water. Drizzle into the wok. Cook for another minute or two or until the sauce has thickened and become smooth. Serve immediately with steamed white rice and lime wedges.

Ginger Scallops

Serves 4

1 tablespoon peanut oil
2 teaspoons minced fresh ginger
1 clove minced garlic
1½ cups whole snow peas/mange tout, fresh or frozen
1 cup carrots, thinly sliced
1lb/500g scallops
1 tablespoon light soy sauce
1/8 teaspoon salt
2 teaspoons cornstarch
¼ cup sliced shallots/spring onions
2 cups hot cooked rice

Heat oil in wok over medium-high heat and add ginger and garlic. Stir-fry for 30 seconds. Add snow peas and carrots and stir-fry a couple of minutes.

Remove vegetables from wok, set aside and keep warm. Add scallops to wok and cook over medium-high heat about 3 minutes, or until scallops are cooked, stirring constantly.

Combine soy sauce, salt and cornstarch, stir well and add to the wok. Add shallots and cook 1 minute, stirring constantly. Add vegetables and serve over hot rice.

Spaghettini and Scallops with Breadcrumbs

Serves 4

12 fresh scallops, with corals (roe)
½ cup extra virgin olive oil
½ cup dried white breadcrumbs
4 tablespoons chopped fresh flat-leaf parsley
2 cloves garlic, finely chopped
1 teaspoon crushed dried chillies
12 oz/375g dried spaghettini
4 tablespoons dry white wine

Detach the corals from the scallops and set aside. Slice the white part of each scallop into 3 or 4 pieces. Heat 2 tablespoons of oil in a frying pan, then add the breadcrumbs and fry, stirring, for 3 minutes or until golden. Remove from the pan and set aside.

Heat 5 tablespoons of oil in the pan, then add half the parsley and the garlic and chilli and fry for 2 minutes or until the flavors are released. Meanwhile, cook pasta in plenty of boiling salted water, until al dente. Drain, return to the saucepan and toss with remaining oil.

Stir-fry the white parts of the scallops for 30 seconds or until they are starting to turn opaque. Add wine and reserved scallop corals and cook for 30 seconds. Add spaghettini and cook for 1 minute, tossing to combine. Sprinkle with breadcrumbs and remaining parsley.

Scallop Stir-Fry

Serves 4

1 tablespoon olive oil
3–4 drops sesame oil
1 medium-sized onion, finely sliced
2 cloves garlic, crushed
1 teaspoon fresh ginger, finely chopped
1 small red capsicum/pepper, sliced
1 small green capsicum/pepper, sliced
1 cup broccoli florets
½ cup bean sprouts
4 shallots/green onions, sliced
1 lb/500g scallops, cut on an angle
1 tablespoon oyster sauce
1 tablespoon light soy sauce
1 fresh chilli or 1 teaspoon of chilli sauce
1½ cups water, thickened with 2 teaspoons cornstarch
20 coriander/cilantro leaves (optional)
boiled rice, to serve

Heat oils in wok or frying pan, add onion, garlic and ginger and stir-fry over medium heat for 30 seconds. Add capsicum, broccoli, sprouts and shallots and stir-fry a further 2 minutes on high heat.

Add scallops and sauces and stir-fry for 1 minute. Pour in cornstarch water and stir until mixture thickens.

Toss in coriander, if using, and serve with boiled rice.

Sichuan-Style Scallops

Serves 4

1½ tablespoons peanut oil
1 tablespoon fresh ginger, finely chopped
1 tablespoon garlic, finely chopped
2 tablespoons shallots/spring onions, finely chopped
1 lb/500g scallops, including corals (roe)
boiled rice for serving

SAUCE
1 tablespoon rice wine or dry sherry
2 teaspoons light soy sauce
2 teaspoons dark soy sauce
2 tablespoons chili bean sauce
2 teaspoons tomato puree
1 teaspoon sugar
½ teaspoon salt
½ teaspoon sugar
2 teaspoons sesame oil

Heat wok until very hot. Add the oil and when it is very hot add the ginger, garlic and shallots. Stir-fry for 10 seconds. Add the scallops and stir-fry for 1 minute.

Add all the sauce ingredients except the sesame oil. Stir-fry for 4 minutes, or until the scallops are firm and thoroughly coated with the sauce.

Add the sesame oil and stir-fry for another minute. Serve immediately with rice.

Prawn/ Shrimp

Preparing Prawns/ Shrimp

Butterflying

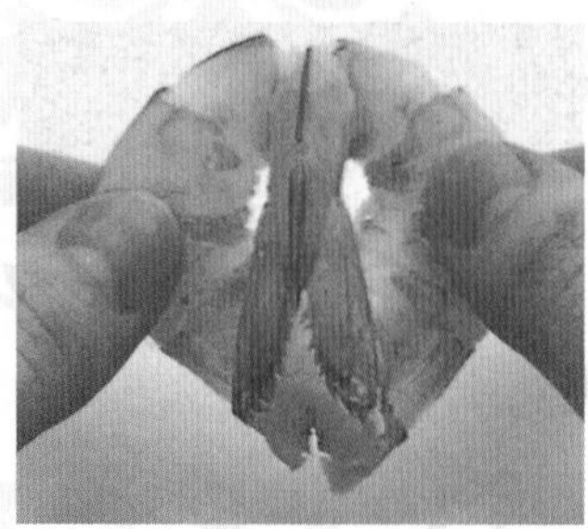

This is usually done on green (uncooked) prawns. It is used to increase both the visual appeal and the size of the prawns.

Cut the peeled prawn lengthwise, almost right through the flesh and along its entire length. This can be done along the stomach, which is the traditional method.

Alternatively, you can cut along the back of the prawn to give a circular shape and larger appearance.

Shelling

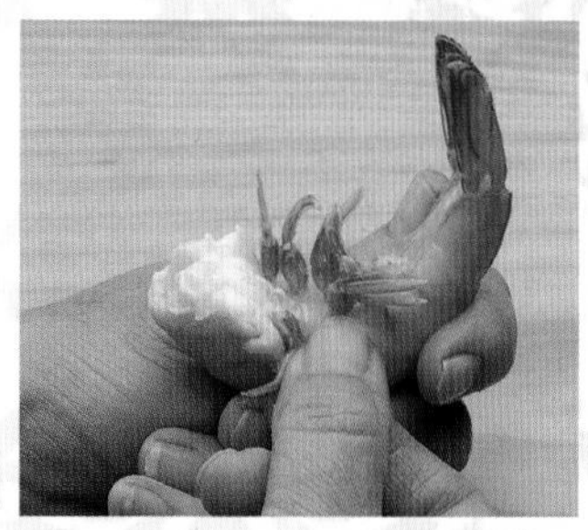

Gently twist the head and pull it from the body.

Using your fingers, roll off the shell from the underside with the legs still attached to the shell.

Gently squeeze the tail and carefully remove the flesh. If you wish, the tail flap can remain attached to the body to enhance presentation.

Deveining

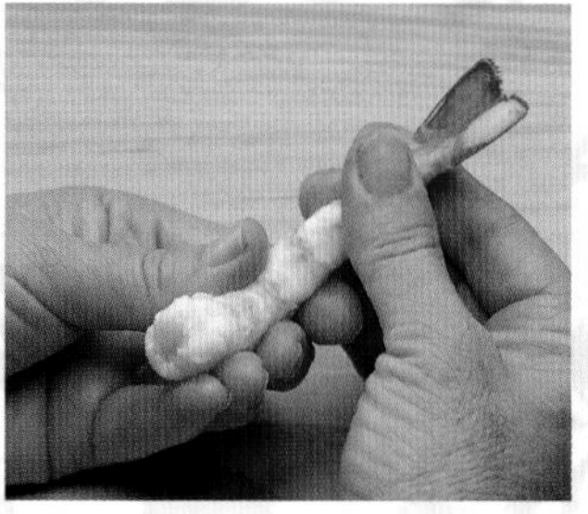

Using your fingers, strip the black intestinal tract (vein) out completely.

For uncooked prawns, you may need to use a small knife to make a shallow cut along the back before removing the intestinal tract.

Shrimp or Prawn?

When is a shrimp a prawn? Is a prawn just a very large shrimp? This perennial question has no consistent answer.

Consult a scientific authority and you'll be told prawns are an entirely different species, related not to shrimp but to the lobster family, with miniature lobster-like bodies 6-8 inches long (15-20cm).

Sound confusing? That's because most of us are more familiar with the designation of prawns as large shrimp although, to add further confusion, even this is not consistent from region to region. In some areas, all shrimp, from small to large, are sold as shrimp (more technically correct). In other areas, only the small and medium crustaceans are called shrimp, while the large ones (15 or fewer to the pound) are called prawns.

In this cookbook, we are using this designation of prawns /shrimp. Most of the recipes specify small, medium or large prawns. If you're still confused, the best thing is to find a knowledgeable local fishmonger. Describe what kind of dish you're preparing, and let your expert advise you about what prawns are freshest and most appropriate for your purpose. You'll soon be an expert in your own right!

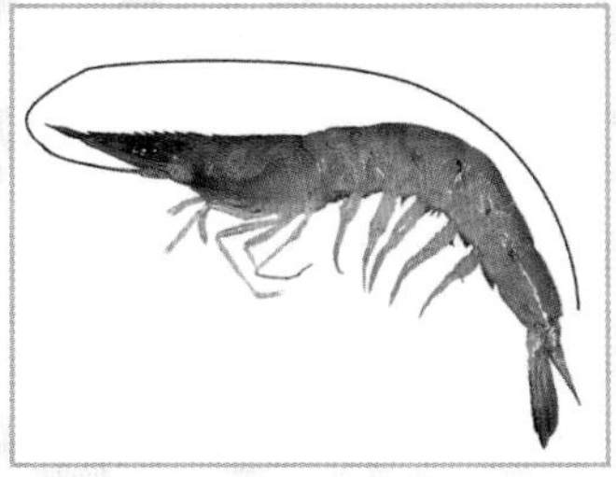

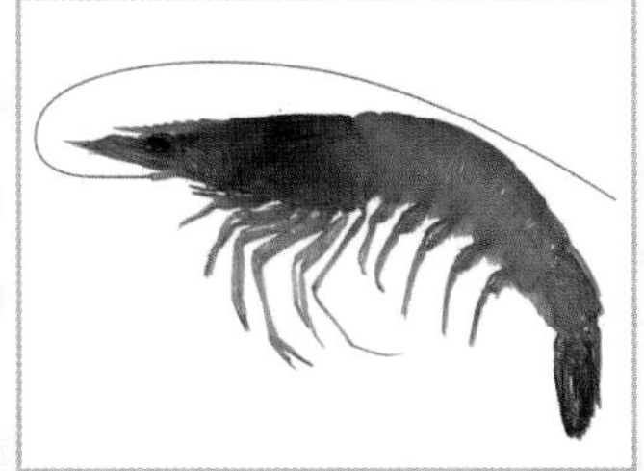

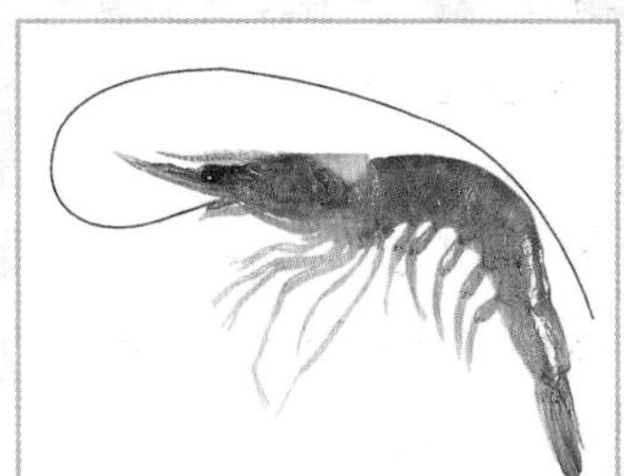

Approximate Cooking Times

Cooking Method	Size	Time
Steaming	Medium – large size	10–15 minutes
	Small – medium size	5–10 minutes
Boiling and Simmering	Large size	5–6 minutes/lb (500g)
	Medium size	3–4 minutes/lb (500g)
Small size	2–3 minutes/lb (500g)	
Deep-frying	Medium size	2–4 minutes
Grilling (all types)	Medium size	2–4 minutes
Microwaving	Per 1/4 lb/125g in marinade	2 minutes

Quality Assessment

Test	Good Quality	Bad Quality
LOOK		
Shell condition	Clean, intact	Damaged, limp appearance
Colour	Bright, glossy	Darkening around the edges of the body segments, legs, shell, flesh, or gut areas Dry, bleached areas Faded, discolored
Head	Firmly attached	Loose, discolored
FEEL		
Flesh	Firm	Soft, slimy, gritty
SMELL	Mild, very slight prawn odor, sea smell	Sweet "off" smell, developing to a strong prawn smell, chemical or ammonia smell

Buying and Storage

- Green (raw unshelled) prawns are available either whole or peeled and deveined, both fresh and frozen. Cooked prawns are available whole, shelled and deveined. For green prawns, look for a firm body with moist flesh and the shell to be tight and intact.
- Do not refreeze green prawns that have been frozen. If you plan to use prawns by the next day after purchase, all you need to do is remove prawns from plastic bag, place in a bowl, cover lightly and place in the coolest part of the refrigerator. If, however, it will be a couple of days and you don't want to freeze them, the following are the best ways to store prawns.
- Green prawns — place in a bowl of ice water, refreshing with ice when it melts, and use within 2 days.
- Cooked prawns — place on a bowl of ice, refreshing when ice melts. Don't allow to sit in water as flavours will be leeched out. Use within 2 days.
- Leave all prawns in their shell. This protects them against dehydration.
- To freeze green prawns, place them in a plastic container covered with water; do not add salt. Cover and freeze. The water forms an ice block that protects the prawns from freezer burn. To thaw, place in the refrigerator for 24 hours. You can freeze for up to 3 months.

Hot and Sour Soup

Serves 4

2 lb/1kg medium uncooked prawns/ shrimp
1 tablespoon vegetable oil
8 slices fresh or bottled galangal or fresh ginger
8 kaffir lime leaves
2 stalks fresh lemon grass, bruised,
2 red chillies, halved and de-seeded, plus 1 red chilli extra, chopped
8 cups water
3 tablespoons chopped coriander/ cilantro leaves
2 tablespoons lime juice
shredded kaffir lime leaves

Shell prawns and devein. Reserve heads and shells. Heat oil in a large saucepan over a high heat, add prawn heads and shells and cook, stirring, for 5 minutes or until shells change colour. Stir in galangal or ginger, lime leaves, lemon grass, halved chillies and water, cover and bring to a simmer. Simmer, stirring occasionally, for 15 minutes.

Strain liquid into a clean saucepan and discard solids. Add prawns and cook for 2 minutes. Stir in coriander, chopped chilli and lime juice and cook for 1 minute or until prawns are tender.

Ladle soup into bowls and garnish with shredded lime leaves.

American Shrimp Bisque

Serves 4

1/3 cup butter
3 tablespoons finely chopped onion
1 stalk celery, finely chopped
1 tablespoon plain/all-purpose flour
2 lb/1kg cooked prawns/shrimp, shelled, deveined and chopped
3½ cups warm milk
½ cup thick or whipping cream
2 tablespoons sherry
salt
freshly ground black pepper
paprika
freshly grated nutmeg
3 tablespoons chopped fresh parsley or snipped chives
serve with crusty bread

Melt butter in a saucepan over low heat, add onion and celery, cover and cook for 5 minutes, taking care not to let vegetables brown.

Stir in flour and cook for 1 minute. Add prawns. Gradually stir in milk until blended. Bring to the boil, lower heat and cook, stirring, for 2 minutes or until soup thickens. Stir in cream and heat through without boiling.

Stir sherry into soup and season to taste with salt, black pepper, paprika and nutmeg. Garnish servings with parsley or chives. Serve with crusty bread.

Spicy Soup

Serves 4

Place stock in a large saucepan and bring to the boil over a medium heat. Add galangal, lime leaves, lemon grass, lime juice, lime rind, fish sauce and curry paste and simmer, stirring occasionally, for 10 minutes.

Add prawns and shallots and simmer for 5 minutes longer or until prawns are cooked.

Remove galangal and discard. Sprinkle soup with coriander and sliced chilli and serve.

4 cups fish stock
2 in/5cm piece fresh galangal, sliced or 8 pieces dried galangal
8 kaffir lime leaves
2 stalks fresh lemon grass, finely chopped
2 tablespoons lime juice
2 tablespoons finely sliced lime rind
2 tablespoons Thai fish sauce (nam pla)
2 tablespoons Thai red curry paste
1 lb/500g uncooked large prawns/shrimp, shelled and deveined, tails left intact
3 shallots/spring onions, sliced diagonally
3 tablespoons chopped coriander/cilantro
1 small fresh red chilli, sliced

Tom Yam Gong

Serves 4

3 cups fish stock
1 tablespoon chopped fresh lemon grass
½ teaspoon finely grated lemon rind
2 tablespoons Thai fish sauce
8 oz/225g button mushrooms, sliced
1 lb/500g large uncooked prawns/shrimp, shelled and deveined
⅓ cup coconut cream
4 oz/115g bean sprouts
2 shallots/spring onions, cut into ¾ ins/2cm lengths
1 teaspoon chilli paste (sambal oelek)
⅓ cup lemon juice
3 tablespoons chopped fresh coriander/cilantro
freshly ground black pepper

Place stock in a large saucepan and bring to the boil. Stir in lemon grass, lemon rind, fish sauce, mushrooms and prawns and cook for 3–4 minutes or until prawns turn red.

Reduce heat to low, stir in coconut cream and cook for 2–3 minutes or until heated through.

Remove pan from heat, add bean sprouts, shallots, chilli paste (sambal oelek), lemon juice, coriander and black pepper to taste. Serve immediately.

Wonton Soup

Serves 6–8

To make wontons, place pork, egg, shallots, chilli, soy sauce and oyster sauce in a bowl and mix to combine.

Place spoonfuls of mixture in the middle of each spring roll or wonton wrapper, then draw the corners together and twist to form small bundles. Place wontons in a steamer set over a saucepan of boiling water and steam for 3—4 minutes or until wontons are cooked.

Place chicken stock in a saucepan and bring to the boil over a medium heat. Add carrot, celery and the capsicum and simmer for 1 minute. Add prawns and cook for 1 minute longer.

To serve, place 3–4 wontons in each soup bowl and carefully ladle over soup. Serve immediately.

PORK WONTONS
8oz/225g ground pork
1 egg, lightly beaten
2 shallots/green onions, chopped
1 fresh red chilli, de-seeded and chopped
1 tablespoon soy sauce
1 tablespoon oyster sauce
24 spring roll or wonton wrappers, each 5 ins/121/2cm square

10 cups chicken stock
1 carrot, cut into thin strips
1 stalk celery, cut into thin strips
1/2 red capsicum/pepper, cut into thin strips
24 large cooked prawns/shrimp, shelled and deveined

Barbecued Marinated

SERVES 8

Preheat barbecue to medium heat.

To make marinade, place chillies, garlic, oregano, parsley, oil, vinegar and black pepper to taste in a bowl and mix to combine.

Add prawns, toss to coat and marinate for 10 minutes.

Drain prawns and cook on oiled barbecue for 1–2 minutes each side or until prawns just begin to redden.

2 lb/1kg uncooked medium prawns/ shrimp, shelled and deveined, tails left intact

CHILLI AND HERB MARINADE

2 fresh red chillies, chopped

2 cloves garlic, crushed

1 tablespoon chopped fresh oregano

1 tablespoon chopped fresh parsley

¼ cup olive oil

2 tablespoons balsamic vinegar

freshly ground black pepper

Hot Chilli

Serves 6

3 lb/1½ kg uncooked large prawns/shrimp, peeled and deveined with tails left intact

CHILLI MARINADE

2 teaspoons cracked black pepper

2 tablespoons sweet chilli sauce

1 tablespoon soy sauce

1 clove garlic, crushed

¼ cup lemon juice

sliced lemon, to serve

MANGO CREAM

1 mango, peeled, pitted and roughly chopped

3 tablespoons coconut milk

To make marinade, place black pepper, chilli sauce, soy sauce, garlic and lemon juice in a bowl and mix to combine. Add prawns, toss to coat, cover and set aside to marinate for 1 hour. Toss several times during marinating.

To make Mango Cream, place mango flesh and coconut milk in a food processor or blender and process until smooth.

Preheat barbecue to a medium heat. Drain prawns and cook on lightly oiled barbecue for 3–4 minutes or until prawns turn red. Serve immediately with Mango Cream and sliced lemon.

Wrapped in Bacon

Serves 4

Place prawns in a medium bowl with the lime juice, garlic, ginger and sugar and mix well. Cover and refrigerate for 30 minutes.

Cut bacon into strips about 1 ins/ 2½cm wide and wrap around each prawn. Thread two prawns onto each skewer.

Grill under a moderate heat for 2 minutes each side or until cooked through.

32 green king prawns/shrimp, peeled and deveined
¼ cup fresh lime juice
1 clove garlic, crushed
1 tablespoon grated fresh ginger
2 tablespoons brown sugar
16 bacon strips, rind removed
16 wooden skewers (soaked in water for 30 minutes)

Sesame Barbecued

Serves 6–8

2 lb/1kg medium–large king prawns/shrimp
¼ cup olive oil
¼ cup red wine
4 eschallots/French shallots, finely chopped
1 teaspoon grated lemon rind
½ teaspoon cracked black pepper
12 bamboo skewers (soaked in water for 30 minutes)
¾ cup toasted sesame seeds
salad, to serve

Peel and devein prawns (leaving the tails intact).

Combine oil, wine, shallots, lemon rind and pepper, mixing well.

Thread the prawns onto bamboo skewers (approximately 3 per skewer).

Place the skewers in a shallow dish and pour marinade over. Allow to marinate for at least 1 hour.

Roll the prawns in the toasted sesame seeds, pressing them on well. Refrigerate for 30 minutes before cooking.

Cook on the hotplate of a well-heated barbecue for 2 minutes each side. Brush with marinade during cooking. Serve with side salad.

Barbecued Chilli

Serves 4

To make marinade, place chilli powder, oregano, garlic, orange and lime rinds and orange and lime juices in a bowl and mix to combine. Add prawns, toss, cover and marinate in the refrigerator for 1 hour.

Drain prawns and cook on a preheated barbecue grill for 1 minute each side or until they turn red.

Place papaya and mint in bowl and toss to combine. To serve, pile prawns onto serving plates, top with papaya mixture and accompany with lime wedges and sliced chillies.

1 kg/2 lb medium uncooked prawns/shrimp, in their shells
1 small papaya, seeded and chopped
2 tablespoons chopped fresh mint
lime wedges
sliced chillies

ORANGE MARINADE

2 tablespoons mild chilli powder
2 tablespoons chopped fresh oregano
2 cloves garlic, crushed
2 teaspoons grated orange rind
2 teaspoons grated lime rind
¼ cup orange juice
¼ cup lime juice

Curry Sesame Kebabs

Serves 6

1 tablespoon vegetable oil
1 tablespoon Madras curry paste
2 tablespoons finely grated fresh ginger
2 cloves garlic, crushed
2 tablespoons lime juice
½ cup plain yogurt
36 uncooked medium prawns/shrimp, shelled and deveined, tails left intact
12 wooden skewers (soaked in water for 30 minutes)
6 tablespoons sesame seeds, toasted
GREEN MASALA ONIONS
2 tablespoons ghee or butter
2 onions, cut into wedges
2 tablespoon green masala paste

Place oil, curry paste, ginger, garlic, lime juice and yogurt in a bowl and mix to combine. Add prawns and toss to coat. Cover and marinate in the refrigerator for 2–3 hours.

Drain prawns and thread 3 prawns onto an oiled skewer. Repeat with remaining prawns to make 12 kebabs. Toss kebabs in sesame seeds and cook on a lightly oiled, preheated medium barbecue or grill for 3 minutes each side or until prawns are cooked.

To make masala onions, melt ghee or butter in a saucepan over medium heat, add onions and cook, stirring, for 5 minutes or until soft. Stir in masala paste and cook for 2 minutes longer or until heated through. Serve with prawns.

Honey and Chilli

Serves 3–4

Mix all ingredients except prawns together to make marinade.

Shell the prawns, leaving on the tails, and devein. Place in a glass dish and add enough marinade to coat well. Cover and marinate in refrigerator for 1 hour. Thread the prawns onto skewers, either through the side or through the length.

Heat the barbecue to medium-high. Place a sheet of foil over the grill bars and place the prawns on the paper. Cook for 4–5 minutes each side: they will turn pink when cooked. Brush with marinade while cooking. Transfer to a platter. If liked, remove prawns from skewers and serve immediately.

¼ cup red wine
½ cup honey
¼ teaspoon ground chilli
1 teaspoon mustard powder
1 lb/500g green king prawns/shrimp
bamboo skewers (soaked in water for 30 minutes)

Teriyaki

Serves 4

2 lb/1kg fresh green prawns/shrimp in shell

TERIYAKI MARINADE

½ cup soy sauce

2 tablespoons brown sugar

½ teaspoon ground ginger

2 tablespoons wine vinegar

1 clove garlic, crushed

2 tablespoons tomato sauce

skewers (if bamboo, soak for 30 minutes prior to using)

To make the marinade, mix all ingredients together and let stand for 1 hour.

Shell the prawns, leaving the tails intact. Place in a non-metal dish and coat with the marinade. Cover and refrigerate for 1 or 2 hours. Thread onto skewers. (For small prawns thread 2 or 3 per skewer. For king prawns thread only one from tail-end to top).

Heat the barbecue and place a square of foil on the grill bars. Place the prawns on the grill, brushing with marinade on both sides as they cook. Cook until prawns turn pink. Take care not to overcook.

Beef with Noodles

Serves 4

5½ oz/155g rice noodles
1 tablespoon peanut oil
2 cloves garlic, crushed
8 oz/250g lean ground/minced beef
8oz/250g uncooked prawns/shrimp, shelled and deveined
2 tablespoons sugar
2 tablespoons white vinegar
1 tablespoon fish sauce
1 fresh red chilli, finely chopped
2 eggs, lightly beaten
1 cup bean sprouts
1 large carrot, grated
3 tablespoons chopped fresh coriander/cilantro
2 tablespoons chopped blanched almonds

Place noodles in a bowl, pour over boiling water to cover and set aside to stand for 8 minutes. Drain well.

Heat oil and garlic in a wok or large frying pan over a high heat, add beef and stir-fry for 2–3 minutes or until meat is brown. Add prawns and stir-fry for 1 minute. Stir in sugar, vinegar, fish sauce, and chilli and bring to boil, stirring constantly.

Add eggs to pan and cook, stirring, until set. Add bean sprouts, carrot and noodles and toss to combine. To serve, sprinkle with coriander and almonds.

Chilli Tempura

Serves 2

vegetable oil for deep-frying
1 lb/500g uncooked large prawns/shrimp, peeled and deveined, tails left intact
12 snow peas/mange tout, trimmed
1 eggplant/aubergine, cut into thin slices
1 small head broccoli, broken into small florets

TEMPURA BATTER
¾ cup self-raising/bakers flour
½ cup cornstarch
1 teaspoon chilli powder
1 egg, lightly beaten
1 cup ice water
4 ice cubes

To make batter, place flour, cornstarch and chilli powder in a bowl, mix to combine and make a well in the middle. Whisk in egg and water and beat until smooth. Add ice cubes.

Heat oil in a deep saucepan until a cube of bread dropped in browns in 50 seconds.

Dip prawns, snow peas, eggplant and broccoli florets in batter and deep-fry a few at a time for 3–4 minutes or until golden and crisp. Serve immediately.

Coconut Salad

Serves 6

2 lb/1kg large raw prawns/shrimp, shelled and deveined, tails left intact
3 egg whites, lightly beaten
1 cup shredded coconut
vegetable oil for deep-frying
1 tablespoon peanut oil
4 fresh red chillies, seeded and sliced
2 small fresh green chillies, seeded and sliced
2 cloves garlic, crushed
1 tablespoon grated fresh ginger
3 kaffir lime leaves, finely shredded
¾ lb/375g scallops
1½ cups snow pea/mange tout leaves or sprouts
2 tablespoons palm or brown sugar
¼ cup lime juice
2 tablespoons Thai fish sauce

Dip prawns in egg whites, then roll in coconut to coat. Heat vegetable oil in a large saucepan until a cube of bread dropped in browns in 50 seconds and cook prawns, a few at a time, for 2–3 minutes or until golden and crisp. Drain on paper towels and keep warm.

Heat peanut oil in a wok over a high heat, add red and green chillies, garlic, ginger and lime leaves and stir-fry for 2–3 minutes or until fragrant.

Add scallops to wok and stir-fry for 3 minutes or until opaque. Add cooked prawns, snow pea leaves or sprouts, sugar, lime juice and fish sauce and stir-fry for 2 minutes or until heated.

Stir-Fry Chilli

Serves 4

1 teaspoon vegetable oil
1 teaspoon sesame oil
3 cloves garlic, crushed
3 fresh red chillies, chopped
2 lb/1kg green medium prawns/shrimp, shelled and deveined
1 tablespoon brown sugar
1/3 cup tomato juice
1 tablespoon soy sauce
snow peas/mange tout and mixed salad to serve

Heat vegetable and sesame oils together in a wok over a medium heat, add garlic and chillies and stir-fry for 1 minute. Add prawns and stir-fry for 2 minutes or until they turn red.

Stir in sugar, tomato juice and soy sauce and stir-fry, for 3 minutes or until sauce is heated through. Serve on snow peas, with mixed green salad.

Thai Garlic

Serves 4

Place garlic, coriander and 2 tablespoons oil in a food processor or blender and process until smooth.

Heat remaining oil in a large wok or frying pan, add garlic mixture and stir-fry for 2 minutes. Add prawns and stir-fry to coat with garlic mixture. Stir in water, fish sauce, sugar and black pepper to taste and stir-fry until prawns are cooked. Serve sizzling hot with lemon wedges.

6 cloves garlic, crushed
6 tablespoons coriander/cilantro
3 tablespoons vegetable oil
1 lb/500g large green prawns, shelled and deveined, tails left intact
¾ cup water
¼ cup fish sauce
1 tablespoon sugar
freshly ground black pepper
lemon wedges, to serve

Ginger Chilli

Serves 4

2 ins/5cm fresh ginger
3 large shallots/spring onions
½ cup peanut oil
½ teaspoon crushed dried chilli
black pepper to taste
1 tablespoon soy sauce
2lb/1kg large green king prawns/ shrimp

Peel the ginger and cut half of it into thin slices. Cut the other half into julienne strips. Cut the shallots (half tops as well) into 2 ins/5cm lengths. Heat oil, add ginger slices, shallots and chilli. Remove from heat, add black pepper and soy sauce and allow to infuse until completely cool.

Wash and then dry prawns and with small scissors, cut along top of shell and remove dark vein down the back. Leave shell and tail on and remove heads if you prefer. Toss the prawns in the cooled oil mixture and leave to marinate for several hours.

When ready to serve, heat grill until very hot and arrange the prawns on the grilling rack. Sprinkle with oil marinade and half ginger strips and cook until pink, then turn and repeat on other side.

Toasts

Makes 18

1lb/500g peeled cooked prawns/ shrimp, deveined
6 shallots/spring onions, chopped
2 teaspoons grated fresh ginger
2 teaspoons light soy sauce
½ teaspoon sesame oil
2 egg whites
6 slices white bread
½ cup fresh white breadcrumbs
oil for deep frying
coriander/cilantro for garnish

Combine prawns, shallots, ginger, soy sauce and sesame oil in a blender or food processor. Blend until roughly chopped. Add egg whites and blend until combined.

Remove crusts from bread slices, spread them with prawn mixture, then cut each slice into three strips.

Dip prawn-coated side of each bread strip into breadcrumbs. Deep fry bread strips in hot oil until light golden brown. Drain on paper towels and serve at once, with a coriander garnish, if desired.

Tiger Prawns with Asian Dipping Sauce

Serves 2

To make the dipping sauce, mix together all ingredients.

Heat oil in a frying pan, then fry prawns for 3–4 minutes or until pink and cooked through.

Arrange lettuce leaves on 2 serving plates, scatter prawns over and garnish with coriander. Serve with dipping sauce.

1 tablespoon sunflower oil
10 green tiger prawns/shrimp, shelled, deveined, tails intact
4 romaine lettuce leaves
chopped coriander/cilantro to garnish
DIPPING SAUCE
1 clove garlic, crushed
½ teaspoon sugar
few drops of Tabasco
finely grated rind and juice of ½ lime
3 tablespoons sunflower oil
salt and ground black pepper to taste

Lemon Grass Noodle

Serves 4

Wash prawns, leaving shells and heads intact, and place in a shallow glass or ceramic dish.

Place lemon grass, shallots, chillies, garlic, ginger and shrimp paste in a food processor or blender and process until smooth. Add sugar and coconut milk and process to combine. Spoon mixture over prawns, toss to combine, cover and marinate in the refrigerator for 3–4 hours.

Preheat barbecue to a high heat. Drain prawns, place on barbecue and cook, turning several times, for 5 minutes or until prawns turn red. Serve immediately with noodles prepared according to packet directions.

2 lb/1kg uncooked medium prawns/shrimp
3 stalks fresh lemon grass, finely chopped
2 shallots/spring onions, chopped
2 small fresh red chillies, finely chopped
2 cloves garlic, crushed
2 tablespoons finely grated fresh ginger
1 teaspoon shrimp paste
1 tablespoon brown sugar
½ cup coconut milk

Braised with Chinese Greens

Serves 4

1½ lb/750g green prawns/shrimp, shelled and deveined
1 tablespoon Chinese wine or dry sherry
1 teaspoon cornstarch
1 teaspoon soy sauce
5 tablespoons oil
12 snow peas/mange tout
1½ cups choy sum/Chinese flowering cabbage
SEASONING
½ teaspoon salt
½ teaspoon sugar
2 teaspoons soy sauce
1 teaspoon sesame oil

Put prawns into bowl with wine or sherry, cornstarch and soy sauce. Mix well, cover and chill for at least 30 minutes.

Heat 4 tablespoons of the oil in a wok and cook prawns until they turn red. Remove. Add rest of oil to wok and cook vegetables for 2 minutes.

Return prawns to wok and add seasoning. Toss until heated through and serve immediately.

Deep-Fried Chilli Coconut

Serves 4

3 eggs, lightly beaten
½ teaspoon chilli powder
1½ cups breadcrumbs, made from stale bread
1½ cups shredded coconut
24 green prawns/shrimp, shelled, deveined, tail intact
1 cup plain/all-purpose flour
vegetable oil for deep-frying
lime or lemon wedges to serve

Combine eggs and chilli powder in a shallow dish. Combine breadcrumbs and coconut in a separate shallow dish.

Roll prawns in flour to coat thickly. Dip in egg mixture. Roll in breadcrumb mixture to coat.

Heat oil in a saucepan until a cube of bread dropped in browns in 50 seconds. Deep-fry prawns in batches for 2 minutes or until golden and crisp. Drain on paper towels.

Nasi Goreng

Serves 4

¼ cup vegetable oil
1 onion, sliced
3 shallots/spring onions, chopped
8 oz/250g diced pork
4 oz/125g raw prawns/shrimp, shelled
4 cups cooked rice
1 red capsicum/pepper, chopped
3 tablespoons raisins
⅓ cup cashews or peanuts
1 teaspoon chopped fresh red chilli
2 tablespoons soy sauce

CHINESE OMELET
2 eggs
2 teaspoons water
freshly ground black pepper

To make omelet, place eggs, water and black pepper to taste in a bowl and whisk to combine. Heat a lightly greased wok or frying pan over a medium heat, add half the egg mixture and tilt pan to thinly coat base. Cook for 1–2 minutes or until underside is set, flip and cook for 10 seconds. Remove and set aside to cool. Use remaining egg mixture to make a second omelet. Stack omelets, roll up and cut into fine shreds. Set aside.

Heat half the oil in a wok or large frying pan over a medium heat, add onion and shallots and stir-fry for 3–4 minutes or until onion is tender. Add pork and stir-fry for 2–3 minutes. Add prawns and stir-fry for 1–2 minutes longer or until prawns turn red. Remove mixture from pan and set aside.

Heat remaining oil in same pan, add rice, capsicum, raisins, cashews or peanuts, chilli and soy sauce and stir-fry for 2 minutes. Return pork mixture to pan and stir-fry for 1 minute or until heated through. Top with omelet strips and serve immediately.

Chilli Pizza

SERVES 4

Place pizza crust on a lightly greased baking tray, spread with tomato paste and set aside.

Heat oil in a frying pan over a medium heat, add cumin, chillies and garlic and cook, stirring, for 1 minute.

Stir in the lemon juice and the prawns and cook for 3 minutes longer or until prawns start to redden and are almost cooked.

Top pizza base with capsicums, then with prawn mixture, coriander, Parmesan cheese and black pepper to taste. Bake at 370°F/190°C for 20 minutes or until base is crisp and golden.

1 fresh or frozen pizza crust

3 tablespoons tomato paste/purée

2 teaspoons vegetable oil

1 teaspoon ground cumin

3 fresh red chillies, de-seeded and chopped

2 cloves garlic, crushed

2 tablespoons lemon juice

1 lb/500g uncooked prawns/shrimp, shelled and deveined

1 red capsicum/pepper, sliced

1 yellow or green capsicum/bell pepper, sliced

2 tablespoons chopped coriander/cilantro

2 tablespoons grated Parmesan cheese

freshly ground black pepper

Linguine in a Roasted Tomato Sauce

Serves 4

14oz/400g linguine
2 lb/1kg tomatoes
olive oil to drizzle, plus 1/3 cup extra
salt and pepper
7oz/200g green prawns/shrimp, peeled
5¼ oz/150g calamari/squid, cut into rings
7oz/200g firm white fish pieces
3 garlic cloves, crushed
2 onions, diced
1 tablespoon tomato paste (optional)
1/3 cup water
½ bunch parsley, chopped
Parmesan cheese

Cook the linguine in salted boiling water until al dente and set aside.

To roast the tomatoes, preheat the oven to 350°F/180°C. Cut the tomatoes in half and place on a baking tray. Drizzle with olive oil, sprinkle with a little salt and pepper, and roast in the oven for 20–25 minutes.

Place in a food processor and process for a few seconds, but do not over-process. (The mixture should still have texture.)

Heat half the remaining oil in a pan, and sauté the prawns for 2 minutes until just cooked, and remove from the pan. Add the calamari and cook for 2 minutes, before removing from the pan. Adding a little more oil if needed, sauté the fish for a few minutes until just cooked, and remove from the pan.

Heat the remaining oil, and sauté the garlic and onion for a few minutes until cooked. Add the tomato mixture, tomato paste if using, and water, and simmer for 10 minutes. Carefully add the seafood to the sauce, season with salt and pepper, and mix through the chopped parsley.

Serve on top of the linguine and sprinkle with Parmesan cheese.

Spanish Rice with Scampi

Serves 4

3 tablespoons olive oil
1 medium onion, finely chopped
2 fresh calamari/squid, cleaned and finely chopped
1 large ripe tomato, skinned and chopped
1¼ cups short-grain rice
3 cups water
pinch saffron threads
salt and ground pepper, to taste
8–16 fresh or thawed frozen scampi
1 lb/500g green king prawns/shrimp

In a large, heavy, flameproof frying pan heat the oil and gently fry the chopped onion and calamari for about 5 minutes. Add the tomato and cook for a further 5 minutes.

Add rice and stir to mix well with the calamari mixture for a minute or two. Bring water to boil with the saffron, salt and ground pepper and pour over the rice.

Add the shellfish, leaving the scampi either whole or halved and shelling the prawns or leaving them whole and unshelled.

Simmer over gentle heat until rice is cooked. The rice should not be stirred at all during the cooking so that the shellfish sits on top.

Spaghetti Marinara

Serves 4

510g/18 oz spaghetti
2 teaspoons vegetable oil
2 teaspoons butter
2 onions, chopped
2 x 400g/14 oz canned tomatoes, undrained and mashed
2 tablespoons chopped fresh basil or 1 teaspoon dried basil
1/4 cup/60mL/2fl oz dry white wine
12 mussels, scrubbed and beards removed
12 scallops
12 raw prawns/shrimp, shelled and deveined
115g/4 oz calamari/squid rings

Cook the pasta in boiling water in a large saucepan. following the packet directions. Drain, set aside and keep warm.

Heat the oil and butter in a frying pan over medium heat. Add the onions and cook, stirring, for 4 minutes or until the onions are golden.

Stir in the tomatoes, basil and wine and simmer for 8 minutes. Add the mussels, scallops and prawns and cook for 2 minutes longer.

Add the calamari and cook for 1 minute or until the shellfish is cooked. Spoon the seafood mixture over hot pasta and serve immediately.

Butterflied with Garlic, Chilli & Parsley

Serves 6

2 lb/1kg (approx 20) green prawns/shrimp, shelled, deveined, tails intact
2 tablespoons olive oil
1 tablespoon lemon juice
2 cloves garlic, crushed
2 red chillies, de-seeded and finely chopped
2 tablespoons parsley, chopped
oil (for frying)
½ cup plain/all-purpose flour (for coating prawns)
lemon wedges and extra parsley (to garnish)

Cut prawns down the back and remove vein.

Combine oil, lemon juice, garlic, chilli and parsley in a bowl. Add prawns, mix well, and leave to marinate for 2–3 hours.

Heat oil in a large pan, coat prawns with flour, and cook quickly in oil for 2–3 minutes. Drain on absorbent paper towels.

Serve with lemon wedges and parsley.

Jambalaya

SERVES 4

3 strips bacon, cut into pieces
1 large onion, finely chopped
1 green capsicum/bell pepper, diced
1 stalk celery, chopped
3 cloves garlic, crushed
1 cup long-grain rice
1½–3 cups boiling chicken stock
14 oz/398mL can tomatoes, drained and mashed
2 teaspoons Cajun spice mix
1 teaspoon dried thyme
1 lb/500g uncooked medium prawns/shrimp, shelled and deveined
5½ oz/155g smoked ham in one piece, cut into ½ ins/1cm cubes
3 shallots/spring onions, finely chopped

Cook bacon in a frying pan over a medium heat for 5 minutes or until crisp. Remove bacon from pan and drain on paper towels.

Add onion to pan and cook, stirring, for 5 minutes or until onion is soft, but not brown. Add capsicum, celery and garlic and cook for 3 minutes. Add rice and cook, stirring frequently, for 5 minutes or until rice becomes translucent.

Stir in stock, tomatoes, spice mix and thyme and bring to the boil. Cover, reduce heat to low and cook for 15 minutes. Stir in prawns, bacon and ham, cover and cook for 10 minutes longer or until rice is tender and liquid absorbed. Sprinkle with shallots and serve immediately.

Shrimp Creole

SERVES 4

Heat oil in large heavy-based frypan and sauté prawns, onion, green bell pepper and celery for a few minutes until softened. Add chopped tomatoes, fish stock, salt, pepper, cayenne and bouquet garni. Bring to simmer and cook for about 25 minutes.

Scoop away the vegetables and set aside, leaving the liquid in the pan. Reduce the liquid over a moderate heat to about half, then return vegetables along with the prawns.

Simmer for 5 minutes, remove bouquet garni and serve sprinkled with parsley.

¼ cup olive oil
2 lb/1kg green prawns/shrimp, shelled
1 large onion, finely chopped
1 green capsicum/bell pepper
1 large stalk celery
4 large ripe tomatoes, peeled and chopped
2 cups fish stock (or stock made from prawn heads and shells)
salt and freshly ground pepper
pinch cayenne
bouquet garni
chopped parsley

Mexican Salsa

Serves 4

1½ lb/750g large raw prawns/ shrimp, shelled and deveined
2 tablespoons lime juice
2 teaspoons ground cumin
2 tablespoons chopped fresh coriander/cilantro
2 fresh red chillies, chopped
2 teaspoons vegetable oil
4 tortillas or flat bread
AVOCADO SALSA
1 avocado, pitted, peeled and chopped
1 tablespoon lemon juice
½ red capsicum/pepper, chopped
2 shallots/spring onions, chopped
½ teaspoon chilli powder
1 tablespoon fresh coriander/ cilantro

Place prawns, lime juice, cumin, coriander, chillies and oil in a bowl, toss to combine and set aside to marinate for 5 minutes.

To make salsa, place avocado, lemon juice, capsicum, shallots, chilli powder and cilantro in a bowl and mix gently to combine. Set aside.

Heat a non-stick frying pan over a high heat, add prawns and stir-fry for 4–5 minutes or until prawns are cooked. To serve, divide prawns among tortillas or flat bread and top with salsa.

King Prawns in a Sweet Potato Crust

Makes 12–16

PRAWNS

1 lb/500g large raw prawns/shrimp, peeled and deveined

2 shallots/spring onions, finely chopped

1 stalk lemon grass, finely chopped

1 tablespoon fresh ginger, minced

½ bunch coriander/cilantro, finely chopped

1 teaspoon fish sauce

1 tablespoon sweet chilli sauce

BATTER

1 large or 2 small sweet potatoes

½ teaspoon turmeric

1 cup coconut milk

½ cup water

½ cup self-raising/bakers flour

½ cup rice flour

1 tablespoon polenta

2 tablespoons peanut oil

lime wedges for serving

Chop the prawns roughly and mix with the finely chopped shallots, lemon grass, fresh ginger, coriander, fish sauce and sweet chilli sauce. Marinate for 1 hour.

Meanwhile, grate the sweet potato and set aside. In a separate bowl, mix the turmeric, coconut milk, water, flours and polenta. Stir thoroughly to combine, then add the grated sweet potato and set aside until prawns are ready. Combine the prawn mixture with the batter and mix thoroughly.

Heat a frypan with peanut oil and drop spoonfuls of the prawn mixture into the frypan. Cook over a medium-high heat for 3 minutes on each side, or until the underside is crisp and golden. Turn them over and cook the other side.

When cooked, remove the fritters from the frypan. Allow them to cool on a wire rack, or serve immediately with lime wedges.

To reheat, place in a preheated 400°F/200°C oven for 5–10 minutes.

If you do not wish to use shellfish, substitute fresh salmon for the prawns and dice before mixing with the marinade ingredients. Then proceed with the recipe above. A combination of prawns and salmon also works very well.

Lobster & Crab

Crab Preparation

To Store

Wrap the crab in plastic wrap or foil or store in an airtight container in the refrigerator for up to 3 days or you can freeze up to 3 months, providing your freezer operates at -18°C/0°F.

To Prepare a Crab

For green or cooked crabs, insert the point of a knife at the 'seam' area where the top shell meets the base (the opposite side of the eyes). Using a lever action lift off the shell. Wash the inside thoroughly and remove the meat if necessary. Break off the claws and snap with a shellfish cracker to remove the meat, or segment into quarters.

To Cook a Crab

The most humane method to cook live crabs is to place the crab into the freezer for several hours. This method does not freeze the meat but has an anaesthetising effect on the crab. (Never plunge into boiling water as this toughens the meat and the claws can fall off. It is also generally thought to be more painful for the crab). Alternatively, to kill the crab instantly, stab it just behind the eyes with the point of a sharp knife (step 1). Place the crab into cold water, cover the pan and bring to boil. Simmer 5–20 minutes (depending upon size).

The crab is cooked when it turns a bright orange colour. A great way to eat crab is cold with lemon and freshly ground black pepper. The meat is sweet and succulent and requires little else. It goes well with lemon, lime, parsley, coriander/cilantro and thyme and is ideal served with tropical fruits such as mango and papaya, and salad vegetables.

To Clean Crab

Place the crab on its back, and gently fold back the tail flap or apron. Twist and pull the apron off. You will find that the intestinal vein is attached and will pull out along the apron. Discard (step 2). Hold the crab with one hand where the apron was removed. Use the other hand to pry up, tear-off and discard the top shell (step 3). Remove the gills, take out the greyish bag and pull out mandibles from the front of the crab. Hold the body where the legs were attached and apply pressure so that the crab splits in half along the centre of the body. Fold back the halves and twist apart (step 4). Twist off the claws and legs where they join the body. Crack with a hammer or nutcracker to make the meat easy to remove.

Step 1

Step 2

Step 3

Step 4

Lobster Preparation

How to Buy lobster

Lobsters may be purchased live in the shell, or freshly cooked in the shell. When purchased live, lobster should show some movement and the tail should spring back when straightened out. Lobsters that show no movement when handled and have a tail that hangs down straight, are dead and should be discarded.

When handling live lobster, be careful of the claws (if they have any) as they can give you a severe pinch. To protect the handler and to prevent the lobster from harming each other in captivity, the claws are usually immobilised by placing an elastic band around them.

When buying cooked lobster, check that they are a bright 'red-orange' and have a fresh aroma. The tail section should spring back into a curled position after being straightened out.

How to Store

Live lobster should never be placed in fresh water or on ice. Under ideal cool, damp storage conditions, lobster can live out of water for up to 36 hours. They can be stored in your refrigerator for several hours by placing them in a large container covered with damp newspaper or seaweed.

Cooked lobster in the shell can be stored in the refrigerator for up to 2 days if placed in an air-tight covered container. Shucked lobster meat can be refrigerated for 2–3 days.

Live lobsters should never be frozen but cooked lobster freezes well. For best results, the cooked meat should be removed from the shell and placed in plastic containers or freezer bags. Prepare a brine solution of 55g/2oz salt to each litre of fresh water. Pour this over the lobster so that all the meat is covered and a 1cm/1/2in headspace remains.

Whole cooked lobster can be frozen in individual heavy plastic bags. Place the lobster in the bag, being careful that the sharp shell does not puncture the bag, cover with a brine solution, then cover tightly and freeze.

To thaw lobster, place in the refrigerator and allow 18 hours for defrosting. To speed up defrosting time, place the package under cold running water until thawed.

How to Prepare

To cook live lobsters, the most humane way is to place the lobster in the freezer then simmer it as you would a crab. Lobster should be cooked either in clean sea water or salted fresh water. Lobster will cook in 12–20 minutes, depending on the size of the lobster. Once cooked, the lobster should be drained immediately. It can now be served hot or chilled quickly by dipping in cold water.

Step 1

Cleaning Lobster

Hold the lobster right-side-up on a firm surface. Pierce the shell at the centre of the body, behind the head (step 1).

Cut the lobster in half lengthwise and remove and discard the sac near the head, and the intestinal vein in the tail. Remove any roe from the body and reserve for sauces (step 2).

Clean the lobster by rinsing under cold, running water (step 3).

Step 2

Step 3

Crab Salad with Tomato Dressing

Serves 4

To make the dressing, place the tomatoes in a bowl and cover with boiling water. Leave for 30 seconds, then skin, de-seed and cut into small dice. Whisk together the oil and vinegar in a bowl, then whisk in the cream, tarragon and seasoning. Add sugar and Worcestershire sauce to taste, then stir in the tomatoes and cucumber.

Mix together the crabmeat and sliced fennel and stir in 4 tablespoons of the dressing. Arrange the salad leaves together with the crab mixture on plates. Spoon over the remaining dressing, then sprinkle with the chives, chopped fennel top and paprika or cayenne pepper.

2 large dressed crabs (about 250g/9 oz crab meat)
1 large bulb fennel, thinly sliced, and feathery top chopped and reserved to garnish
85g/3 oz mixed salad leaves
1 tablespoon snipped fresh chives and paprika or cayenne pepper to garnish
DRESSING
2 large tomatoes
5 tablespoons olive oil
1 tablespoon white wine vinegar
4 tablespoons cream
1 teaspoon chopped fresh tarragon
salt and black pepper
pinch of caster/superfine sugar
dash of Worcestershire sauce
2 ins/5cm piece cucumber, diced

Lobster with Dill

Serves 4

2 lobsters weighing approx 750g/26 oz each
few sprigs dill
1 lettuce
2 slices fresh or unsweetened canned pineapple
100g/3½ oz button mushrooms
1 tablespoon mayonnaise
200mL/7fl oz whipping cream
pinch sugar
salt and white pepper

Prepare the lobsters for cooking and add to a very large pan of boiling, slightly salted water. Cook for 15–20 minutes. Drain, take all the meat out of the shells and claws, and dice. Wash and dry the dill and snip off the small feathery leaves, reserving a sprig or two for decoration.

Wash and dry the lettuce. Drain the pineapple well and cut into small pieces. Slice the mushrooms wafer thin.

Place all the ingredients except the lettuce and dill in a bowl and mix with the mayonnaise. Fold in the cream, flightly beaten with a pinch of sugar; salt and freshly ground white pepper.

Line a large salad bowl with the lettuce leaves, spoon in the lobster mixture and decorate with the reserved dill sprigs.

Lobster Bisque

Serves 4

1 small lobster, cooked
1 large carrot, peeled and diced
1 small onion, finely chopped
125g/4½ oz butter
¾ cup dry white wine
bouquet garni
6½ cups fish or chicken stock
¾ cup rice
salt, pepper and ground cayenne
½ cup cream
2 tablespoons brandy
chopped parsley

Split the lobster in half lengthwise, and remove the flesh from the shell. Set aside. Wrap the shell in a clean tea towel, crush the shell with a hammer and set aside. Sauté the carrot and onion in half the butter until softened (about 5 minutes). Add the crushed shell, sauté a further minute or so then add the wine. Boil rapidly until reduced by half. Add the bouquet garni, stock and rice.

After about 20 minutes, when the rice is tender, remove the large pieces of shell and the bouquet garni. Purée small batches in a food processor with the remainder of the batter, doing so in small batches. Pour through a strainer. Rinse out the food processor to remove every trace of shell and purée the strained liquid again, this time with the lobster flesh, saving a few pieces for the garnish. Reheat gently.

Taste, add salt, pepper and cayenne to taste then stir in the cream, brandy and reserved lobster pieces, cut into thin slices. Serve very hot garnished with parsley.

Creamy Lobster Chowder

SERVES 4–6

55g/2 oz quick cooking rice
1 teaspoon salt
¼ teaspoon pepper
¼ teaspoon paprika
1 tablespoon onion, finely minced
1 small red capsicum/pepper, diced
2 stalks celery, chopped
2 cups milk
2 cups light cream
370g/13 oz lobster meat, diced
2 tablespoons butter
2 tablespoons parsley, chopped

Combine the rice, salt, pepper, paprika, onion, capsicum, celery, milk and cream in a saucepan. Cook over medium heat, stirring frequently, for 10–12 minutes, or until the rice softens.

Stir in the lobster and butter. Remove from the heat, cool and store in the refrigerator. Just before serving, stir through the parsley then reheat the chowder over medium heat, stirring frequently.

Tarragon Seafood Salad

Serves 4

4 tablespoons chopped fresh tarragon
2 tablespoons lime juice
3 teaspoons grated lime rind
1 fresh red chilli, chopped
2 teaspoons olive oil
freshly ground black pepper, to taste
510g/18 oz uncooked lobster tail, flesh removed from shell and cut into large pieces or 510g/18 oz firm white fish fillets, cut into large pieces
255g/9 oz snow pea/mange tout sprouts or watercress
1 cucumber, sliced into ribbons
2 carrots, sliced into ribbons
1 red capsicum/pepper, cut into thin strips

Place the tarragon, lime juice, lime rind, chilli, oil and black pepper in a bowl and mix to combine. Add lobster, toss to coat and set aside to marinate for 15 minutes.

Arrange the snow pea sprouts or watercress, cucumber, carrot and capsicum on a large serving platter and set aside.

Heat a char-grill or frying pan over a high heat, add the lobster mixture and cook, turning frequently, for 2 minutes or until the lobster is tender. Arrange the lobster over salad, spoon over the pan juices and serve immediately.

To make cucumber and carrot ribbons, use a vegetable peeler to remove strips lengthwise from the cucumber or carrot. This salad is also delicious made using prawns/shrimp instead of lobster. If using prawns, shell and devein them before marinating.

Crab-stuffed Mushrooms

Serves 4

8 mushrooms (each about 2 ins/5cm diameter) stem removed
French dressing, for marinating
200g/7 oz crab meat
2 tablespoons finely chopped red capsicum/pepper
2 tablespoons finely chopped celery
1 teaspoon lemon juice
¼ teaspoon Dijon mustard
chopped fresh dill
2 tablespoons sour cream
3 tablespoons mayonnaise

Marinate the mushrooms in the French dressing for about 30 minutes.

Place the crab meat, capsicum and celery in a bowl. Lightly mix together.

Blend the remaining ingredients together, and mix through the crab mixture. Chill.

Just before serving, drain the mushroom caps and fill with the crab mixture.

Lobster Croquettes

Serves 4

510g/18oz lobster meat
½ teaspoon pepper
½ teaspoon salt
pinch of mace
115g/4 oz breadcrumbs
55g/2 oz butter
1 egg, beaten
6 plain crackers, pulverised
lard, for cooking
chopped parsley, for garnish

Chop the lobster meat, add pepper, salt and a pinch of mace.

Mix with this about a quarter as much breadcrumbs as you have meat. Add enough melted butter to shape them into pointed balls.

Roll in the beaten egg, then in the pulverized crackers, and fry in the boiling lard.

Serve very hot, garnished with the parsley.

Lobster Toasts

SERVES 6

255g/9 oz cream cheese
55g/2 oz unsalted butter
55g/2 oz cooked lobster meat
1 tablespoon olive oil
juice of ½ lemon
salt and pepper, to taste
extra olive oil, for serving
12 slices of French baguette, or Turkish bread, toasted
fresh parsley, chopped, for garnish

Combine all the ingredients, except toast and parsley in a food processor and blend until creamy.

Spread on the toast and heat through under a preheated hot grill before serving.

Sprinkle with chopped parsley and ground black pepper, drizzle with some olive oil and serve.

Scampi with Basil Butter

Serves 4

Cut the scampi or yabbies in half, lengthwise.

To make the basil butter, place the butter, basil, garlic and honey in a small bowl and whisk to combine.

Brush the cut side of each scampi or yabbie half with basil butter and cook under a preheated hot grill for 2 minutes or until the shells turn red and are tender.

Drizzle with any remaining basil butter and serve immediately.

8 uncooked scampi or yabbies, heads removed

BASIL BUTTER

85g/3 oz butter, melted

2 tablespoons chopped fresh basil

1 clove garlic, crushed

2 teaspoons honey

Sea Captain's Dip

Makes 2 cups

115g/4 oz cream cheese
2 tablespoons lemon juice
55mL/2fl oz mayonnaise
¼ teaspoon garlic salt
2 tablespoons onion, diced
1 teaspoon dried chives
170g/6 oz lobster meat, finely diced

Cream the cream cheese and lemon juice. Add the mayonnaise, garlic salt, onion, chives and lobster and mix well.

Chill at least for 6 hours, then serve with crackers or fresh vegetables.

Lobster Crêpes

Serves 6

If frozen, thaw and chop the lobster into bite-sized pieces. Melt the butter and sauté the onions and the mushrooms for 3–5 minutes. Stir in the flour and seasonings, add the milk and cook, stirring constantly until thickened. Add the lobster.

To make the crêpes, beat the eggs, add the flour and seasonings. Add the milk and beat until smooth. Refrigerate for 2 hours. For each crêpe, pour 2–3 tablespoons of batter into a heated, oiled pan. Brown lightly on each side.

Spoon 3 tablespoons of filling into each crêpe, roll up and arrange in a baking dish. Brush with half the melted butter and sprinkle with the grated cheese. Bake at 220°C/425°F for 5–8 minutes. Stir the remaining melted butter into the remaining filling and serve over the crêpes.

FILLING

510g/18 oz lobster meat, fresh or frozen
55g/2 oz butter
2 tablespoons onion, chopped
455g/16 oz mushrooms, sliced
55g/2oz flour
½ teaspoon salt
1/6 teaspoon pepper
1 cup milk
55g/2 oz butter, melted
55g/2 oz Swiss cheese, grated

CRÊPES

2 eggs
170g/6oz flour
½ teaspoon salt
1 teaspoon dried parsley
1 teaspoon dried chives
1 cup milk

Grilled Scampi with Herb Butter

Serves 4

10–12 scampi or yabbies
140g/5 oz butter
few sprigs fresh herbs, chopped
2 tablespoons chopped parsley
2 cloves garlic, finely chopped
salt and freshly ground pepper
lemon wedges, to serve

Split the scampi or yabbies lengthwise and arrange, cut side up, on a large shallow dish. Melt the butter and add the herbs and garlic. Drizzle butter mixture over the scampi and season with freshly ground pepper. (The scampi can be prepared ahead up to this stage.)

Preheat the griller and arrange the scampi, cut side up, on the grilling pan. Cook for about 5 minutes until the flesh has turned white. Remove from the heat, season with salt and arrange on a large serving platter with wedges of lemon. To eat the scampi use a fork to pull out the tail meat.

Place a bowl on the table for the discarded shells, and a few finger bowls, each with a squeeze of lemon.

Grilled Lobster with Chilli Salsa

Serves 2

To make the salsa, heat the oil in a saucepan and fry the capsicum, onion and chilli for 5 minutes or until tender. Stir in the tomato paste and season to taste. Transfer to a bowl.

To cut lobsters in half lengthways, cut through head end first, using a large, sharp knife, then turn the lobster around and cut through the tail end. Discard the small greyish 'sac' in the head—everything else in the shell is edible. Crack the large claws with a small hammer or wooden rolling pin. Repeat with the second lobster. Drizzle the cut side of the lobsters with the oil and sprinkle with the cayenne pepper.

Heat a large non-stick frying pan or ridged cast iron grill pan until very hot, then add the lobster halves, cut-side down, and cook for 2–3 minutes, until lightly golden. Serve with the salsa.

2 cooked lobsters (about 340g/12 oz each)
4 teaspoons olive oil
cayenne pepper

SALSA
2 tablespoons olive oil
1 red capsicum/pepper, de-seeded and diced
1 small onion, chopped
1 large red chilli, de-seeded and finely chopped
1 tablespoon sun-dried tomato paste
salt and black pepper

Bouillabaisse

Serves 6

3kg/6½ lb mixed fish and seafood, including firm white fish fillets, prawns/shrimp, mussels, crab and calamari/squid rings
55mL/2fl oz olive oil
2 cloves garlic, crushed
2 large onions, chopped
2 leeks, sliced
2 x 400g/14 oz canned tomatoes, undrained and mashed
1 tablespoon chopped fresh thyme
2 tablespoons chopped fresh basil
2 tablespoons chopped fresh parsley
2 bay leaves
2 tablespoons finely grated orange rind
1 teaspoon saffron threads
1 cup dry white wine
1 cup fish stock
freshly ground black pepper

Remove the bones and skin from the fish fillets and cut into ¾ ins/ 2cm cubes. Peel and devein the prawns (shrimp), leaving the tails intact. Scrub and remove the beards from the mussels. Cut the crab into quarters. Set aside.

Heat the oil in a large saucepan over a medium heat, add the garlic, onions and leeks and cook for 5 minutes or until the onions are golden. Add the tomatoes, thyme, basil, parsley, bay leaves, orange rind, saffron, wine and stock and bring to the boil. Reduce the heat and simmer for 30 minutes.

Add the fish and crab and cook for 10 minutes. Add the remaining seafood and cook for 5 minutes longer or until the fish and seafood are cooked. Season to taste with black pepper.

Crab with Ginger

Serves 4

2 x 750g/26 oz or 1 x 1.5kg/3$^{1}/_{3}$ lb fresh mud crab
1 tablespoon corn oil
55g/2 oz fresh peeled ginger, thinly sliced and cut into strips
1 teaspoon crushed garlic
5 eschallots/French shallots, cut into 2 ins/5cm pieces
1 cup fish stock
1 tablespoon dry sherry
1 teaspoon oyster sauce
½ teaspoon Worcestershire sauce
1 tablespoon soy sauce
½ teaspoon sugar
2 teaspoon cornflour, mixed with 1 tablespoon cold water
1 teaspoon sesame oil
1 red chilli, slivered, for garnish
boiled rice, for serving

Steam the crab for 8 minutes over vigorously boiling water. Remove the crab, let cool, then remove the top shell and clean. Cut the body in half and remove the legs and claws. Set aside.

Preheat a wok or large skillet, then heat the oil, add ginger and stir-fry until the ginger is fragrant (about 30 seconds).

Add the garlic and eschallots with the crab pieces, and stir-fry for about 1 minute.

Combine the stock, sherry, oyster sauce, Worcestershire sauce, soy sauce and sugar, and pour into the wok. Cover and cook over medium heat for 3 minutes.

Remove the crab with tongs, and set aside on plate.

Add the dissolved cornflour to the wok and cook, stirring, until the sauce thickens (about 1 minute).

Pour the sauce and eschallot mixture onto a serving platter, reassemble the crab, and place the shell over the body to give the impression of a whole crab lying on the platter.

Trickle sesame oil over the surface, garnish with chilli slivers, and serve with boiled rice on the side.

Sherried Crab Vol-au-Vents

Serves 4–6

255g/9 oz mushrooms
3 tablespoons butter, plus 2 tablespoons butter, extra
3 tablespoons flour
1 cup chicken stock
115mL/4fl oz cream
510g/18 oz crab meat, flaked
55g/2 oz Parmesan cheese
55g/2 oz baby spinach leaves
½ red capsicum/pepper, finely diced
salt and cracked black peppercorns
2 tablespoons dry sherry
vol-au-vent cases

Sauté the mushrooms in 2 tablespoons of the butter, and set aside.

Melt the extra butter and stir in the flour. Cook, stirring, for 2 minutes.

Over low heat, stir in the chicken stock and cream. When the sauce is boiling, add the crab meat and mushrooms.

When the sauce comes to boil again, add the Parmesan cheese, spinach and capsicum and season with salt and pepper.

Remove from the heat and add the sherry. Spoon into heated vol-au-vent cases.

Fresh Crab Tagliatelle

Serves 4

340g/12 oz dried tagliatelle
3 tablespoons olive oil
2 cloves garlic, chopped
1 red chilli, de-seeded and chopped
finely grated rind of 1 lemon
2 fresh dressed crabs, to give about 315g/ 11 oz crab meat
200mL/7fl oz single cream
1 tablespoon lemon juice
salt and black pepper
2 tablespoons chopped fresh parsley, to garnish

Cook the pasta according to the instructions on the packet, until tender but still al dente, then drain.

Meanwhile, heat the oil in a large heavy-based frying pan and gently fry the garlic, chilli and lemon rind for 3–4 minutes, until softened but not browned. Add the crab meat, cream and lemon juice and simmer for 1–2 minutes to heat through. Season to taste.

Transfer the pasta to serving bowls. Spoon the crab mixture over the top and sprinkle with the parsley to garnish.

Chilli Crab

Serves 4

2 medium or 1 large crab, or 6 blue swimmer crabs
3 tablespoons vegetable oil
1 tablespoon lemon juice
salt

SAUCE
2–3 red chillies, seeded and chopped
1 onion, peeled and chopped
2 cloves garlic, peeled and chopped
2 teaspoons grated fresh ginger
2 tablespoons vegetable oil
2 ripe tomatoes, skinned, seeded and chopped, or 2 teaspoons tomato paste
1 teaspoon sugar
1 tablespoon light soy sauce
3 tablespoons water

Clean the crabs thoroughly, then cut each body into 2 or 4 pieces. Chop or crack the claws into 2 or 3 places if they are large. Heat the oil in a frying pan, add the crab pieces and fry for 5 minutes, stirring constantly. Add the lemon juice and salt to taste, remove from the heat and keep hot.

To make the sauce, put the chillies, onion and garlic with ginger in a blender and work to a smooth paste. Heat the oil in a wok or deep frying pan. Add spice paste and fry for 1 minute, stirring constantly. Add the tomatoes, sugar and soy sauce and stir-fry for 2 minutes, then stir in the water. Add salt if necessary and simmer for a further 1 minute. Add the crab and stir to coat each piece in the sauce and cook the crab through, for only 1–2 minutes. Serve hot.

Lobster Lasagne

Serves 10–12

8 fresh lasagne sheets, prepared according to packet directions
255g/9 oz chopped onion
30g/1 oz butter
225g/8 oz cream cheese, softened
1 egg, beaten
310g/11 oz chopped dill pickles
2 teaspoons chopped basil
285mL/10fl oz cans cream of mushroom soup
½ cup milk
85mL/3fl oz white wine or chicken broth
85mL/3fl oz seafood sauce
310g/11 oz fresh or canned lobster meat, thawed and drained (several pieces of lobster meat can be set aside for a garnish, if desired)
285g/10 oz scallops, thawed if frozen and cut in half
85g/3 oz grated Parmesan cheese
255g/9 oz mozzarella cheese

Arrange 4 lasagne sheets to cover the bottom of an oiled 9 x 13 ins/23 x 33cm baking dish. Sauté the onion in the butter just until tender. Stir in the cream cheese, egg, pickles and basil, mixing well. Spread half of this cheese mixture over the lasagne sheets.

Preheat oven to 180°C/350°F. Combine the soup, milk, wine, seafood sauce, lobster and scallops and fold over until well mixed. Spread half over the cheese mixture in the dish. Repeat layers with the remaining lasagne, cheese and seafood mixture. Sprinkle with Parmesan.

Place in oven and bake uncovered for 40 minutes or until heated through. Sprinkle with mozzarella and bake for 2–3 minutes longer or until the cheese melts. Remove from the oven and let stand for 15 minutes before serving.

Grilled Creamy Lobster

Serves 6

Halve the lobsters lengthwise and remove the meat. Cut into chunks and set aside. Melt the butter and sauté the onions until tender. Add the flour and stir over a low heat for 2 minutes. Gradually add the milk and allow the sauce to thicken.

Add the liqueur and simmer for 2 minutes then stir in the cheese and mustards. Spoon a little of the sauce into the lobster shells, add the lobster and coat with the remaining sauce. Sprinkle with breadcrumbs and dot with butter. Place under a pre-heated hot grill until brown and bubbling. Serve immediately.

3 medium, cooked lobsters
45g/1½ oz butter or margarine
1 small onion, chopped
3 tablespoons flour
340mL/12fl oz milk
3 tablespoons cherry liqueur
2 tablespoons grated mild cheddar cheese
2 teaspoons French mustard
½ teaspoon English mustard
breadcrumbs
extra butter

Lobster Mornay

Serves 2

1 medium lobster cooked and halved
MORNAY SAUCE
310mL/11fl oz milk
1 bay leaf
1 small onion, chopped
5 black peppercorns
30g/1 oz butter, plus 15mL/½ fl oz extra, melted
2 tablespoons plain flour
65mL/2¼ fl oz cream
65g/2¼ oz cheese, grated
salt and cracked black peppercorns
65g/2¼ oz fresh breadcrumbs
lemon wedges and salad, to serve

Remove the lobster meat from the shells, reserve shells. Cut lobster meat into bite-sized pieces and set aside.

In a saucepan, place the milk, bay leaf, onion and peppercorns. Heat slowly to boiling point. Remove from the heat, cover and stand for 10 minutes. Strain.

In a pan, heat the butter, then remove from the heat. Stir in the flour and blend, gradually adding the strained milk. Return the pan to the heat, and stir constantly until the sauce boils and thickens. Simmer the sauce for 1 minute. Remove from the heat, add the cream, cheese, salt and pepper. Stir the sauce until the cheese melts, and add the lobster meat.

Divide the lobster and sauce mixture between the shells. Melt extra butter in a small pan, add the breadcrumbs, and stir to combine.

Pour the butter and crumbs over the lobster and brown under a preheated hot grill. Serve with lemon wedges and salad.

Lobster Newburg

Serves 4–6

55g/2oz butter
2kg/4½ lb lobster, boiled, shelled and cut into small pieces
2 teaspoons salt
¼ teaspoon ground cayenne pepper
¼ teaspoon ground nutmeg
1 cup double cream
4 egg yolks
2 tablespoons brandy
2 tablespoons dry sherry
reserved lobster-tail shell or 4–6 vol-au-vent cases
rice, for serving
asparagus spears, to serve

In a shallow frying pan melt the butter over a moderate heat. When the foam subsides, add the lobster.

Cook slowly for about 5 minutes. Add the salt, cayenne pepper and nutmeg.

In a small bowl lightly beat the cream with the egg yolks. Add the mixture to the pan, stirring continuously.

Finally, add the brandy and sherry as the mass begins to thicken. Do not allow to boil or the sauce will curdle.

Serve either placed back in the lobster tail shell or in vol-au-vent cases. Serve with steamed rice and asparagus spears.

Chinese Lobster Stir-fry

Serves 4

510g/18 oz lobster meat, fresh or frozen
1 small clove garlic, minced
2 tablespoons oil
½ cup chicken stock
1 small red capsicum/pepper
255g/9 oz bean sprouts
255g/9 oz water chestnuts
255g/9 oz broccoli
370g/13 oz Chinese cabbage (wombok), chopped
½ teaspoon salt
¼ teaspoon pepper
1 egg, lightly beaten

If frozen, thaw and chop the lobster into bite sized pieces. In a skillet, sauté the lobster and garlic in the oil for 1 minute. Add the stock and vegetables and simmer, uncovered, for 5 minutes. Season with salt and pepper.

Add a little of the hot stock to the beaten egg. Stir the egg mixture into the vegetables and lobster. Heat gently but do not boil. Serve with rice.

Index